MW00610858

THE RESTLESS PEN

A GIFT FROM AN AGELESS GENERATION

by

WRITERS GROUP
OF
LEISURE WORLD

Copyright © 2022 by Writers Group of Leisure World

All rights reserved

Paperback IBSN: 978-1-7346579-5-1

eBook IBSN: 978-1-7346579-6-8

Library of Congress Control Number: 2022913315

Contact an author at WritersofLW@gmail.com

Printed in the United States of America

*To all those who nurtured
the birth and growth of our
Writers Group of Leisure World
and
To our families.*

Another book by Writers Group of Leisure World:

Lessons of Life - Wisdom from an Ageless Generation

ISBN: 978-1-7346579-2-0

Poems and essays capture the life experiences of 15 talented authors from diverse backgrounds

CONTENTS

Redemption
A Memory of My Third Christmas
The Hun Named Attila
The Corner of the Living Room

First Date
Nature Walks
The Fall Season
Winter Wonderland Adventures
Once There Was an Accident
It Was a Dark and Stormy Night
The Blue Straw Hat
One Sunny Day
Our Unexpected Snowstorm
Springtime Shuttle Ride
The First Hat
Wandering Thoughts
Car Excitement
Reflections (Butterflies)
Childhood Menagerie
Springtime in Maryland
Jill's Windy Wedding

A Man from Uncle
A Way Out
This Competition is Criminal
The Greatest Thrill in Sports

Study in Blue and Green
Dead Man's Mountain

by Kenneth V. Cummins

My Field of Dreams
Yes, Dogs Have Souls!
Man's Best Friend
At the Mailbox
High School Albatross

INTRODUCTION

You are about to plunge into icy water, gasping for air and struggling to avoid panic.

You are about to curl up with a book of poems to touch the heart and stimulate the mind.

You are about to hit a homerun, behold the wonders of spring, work alongside the most famous anthropologist in the world, dodge bullets, find love, lose love, and find it again.

Inside these pages are the natural, the supernatural, and the unnatural. You will find truth and fiction, courage and fear, mystery and serenity, sadness and laughter.

The stories within have one point in common - - each of the authors and poets has spent more than four decades perfecting their craft.

With great humility we present to you, "The Restless Pen - A Gift from an Ageless Generation" on behalf of the Writers Group of Leisure World.

May our words lighten your spirit, move your sensibilities to positive action, open your mind to new perspectives, and fill your heart with love.

Sincerely,
Writers Group of Leisure World
Silver Spring, Maryland

♦ ♦ ♦ ♦ ♦

CHAPTER 1

LOVE POEMS

By Danuta Montorfano

My Mother's Garden

She loved the Plant Kingdom
And revered Nature, as her ancestors did.
Fruit trees, bushes and flowers
Surrounded her house.

In the front garden,
Concealed by an evergreen hedge,
The fragrance of orange blossoms
Permeated the air.
Calla lilies and violas were everywhere
And a small banana tree, with its large leaves,
Made you day-dream about the tropics.

By the fence there were roses,
Red, pink and white.
Some of their branches were reaching for the beams
  of light
That filtered through the dense foliage;
Busy bees and an occasional hummingbird
Would liven up that beautiful rose garden.

In the back patio a pergola, with hanging grapes,
Led to the vegetable patch
Where carrots, horseradish and herbs intermingled,
And the tomatoes ripened under the sun.

When severe pains would strike her
She would rush, shovel in hand,
To work on her land.

Her garden gave her joy
Until the end of her life.
It was her small parcel of paradise
On the earth that she loved so much.

Edelweiss in Exile

"Oh beautiful,
Small white flower of the Alps.
So difficult to find
Even by the best mountaineers.

Far away and long, long ago,
As a small girl, I saw you
On a mountain top.
And was fascinated by your beauty.

You were like an apparition.
I touched you
And caressed your wooly and velvety hairs
With my fingertips;
A sensation I never forgot."

Then, one day, also long ago,
I saw you in a nursery
And could not resist buying you.

At home, I planted you
Outside my bedroom window,
In a small rock and moss garden.

You survived for one year
And later faded away.
I think you missed the mountains
And your sisters of the valley.

Yet your memory lives on,
Engraved in some Austrian coins
And in the imagination of dreamers.

Sleepy Town II (Blizzard of 2016)

Old man winter casts a spell.
A heavy mantle of snow covers
The whole town.
Buries cars and streets,
Sidewalks become impassable.
Winter wonderland in parks and country.
Sleepy town, sleepy town.

Breaking the all-around silence,
A few birds hopping and chirping
On the snow by the front door,
Searching for food
And flying from tree to tree.

While snowflakes keep falling
And continuing their dance macabre.
Sleepy town, sleepy town,
When will you come out of hibernation?

Lone Walker

Hot summer evening,
Dark and cloudy sky.
All is so calm...
Floating around,
By the bushes and trees,
Fireflies flashing lights.

There is no one else walking
On the sidewalks or streets.
Houses are lit,
Reminding me of Magritte's painting.
I think: Does art imitate Nature
Or Nature looks like art?

Street lights are on,
And as I head home,
Walking downhill,
Do I have a companion?
No! The long shadow ahead of me
Is my own

Afternoon in Como

Walking along the shore of the lake
With my little daughter
We stop at the candy shop
And then at a park and at a small zoo.

She is fascinated by the little chimpanzees
Bouncing and swinging from the branches of a small tree
And, napping in a corner,
A small Binturong, an exotic Asian black bear.

I treasure that small scale image
Of a little girl watching with awe
Small animals in a small zoo,
By that beautiful emerald lake
In the shadow of the Alps in Lombardy,
Very near the place
Where some of her ancestors came from.

With the beauty all around us,
And my daughter hand in hand,
This was an unforgettable trip.

The Boulevard of Yellow Flowers

Yellow dominates this week of spring.
Rows and rows of daffodils
In the gardens and the yards.
The beautiful color of these flowers
Fills my heart with joy.

In some gardens, clumps of them
Stand like bouquets, displaying their coronas.
There is an abundance of pansies
Along the curbs, themselves painted yellow.
Further up on the hills, bushes of forsythias in full bloom
Looking like walls of little fortresses.

In the sky, the clouds are outlined
By the golden glow of the setting sun.
So much yellow everywhere reminds me
Of paintings of Van Gogh
And the luminosity of Turner's landscapes.

An avalanche of memories flow through my mind:
A yellow polka dot bikini that I wore when I was young;
The yellow "cabs" of New York City;
The yellow Ferrari in the parking lot of a supermarket in
    Long Island
(Once I joked that it was mine, but one is allowed to
    dream, isn't one?)
Yellow roses and nasturtiums in my mother's garden.

Also my children's golden hair when they were little,
And the dandelion flowers they picked from the lawn
And then brought to me: "Mommy, this is for you!"

Many happy memories revived while walking
On the path along the Boulevard, this spring day,
In the midst of this glorious yellow landscape.

Separate Beds

A married couple
Shared and enjoyed
Their queen size bed
For many, many years.

Then, one day, a dark cloud
Crossed the sky and that normal,
Happy situation came to an end.
The husband, like Don Quijote,
Started to fight windmills in his dreams.
He was protecting his family, he thought.

It was all dreams,
But the fights were real.

His wife decided on separate beds.
Each one in its own.
Now, when sleep comes,
He still acts up his nightmarish dreams
But she feels safer in her bed.

Autumn Day

Gray and misty day;
Many trees are dressed in orange
And shades of yellow.
Some have shed their leaves,
That are lying like beautiful minicarpets
On the ground ...

Other leaves, dry and brown, gather
On the sidewalks and curbs.
And one can see imprints of maple and oak leaves
Etched on the cement.

An occasional falling acorn breaks the silence.
A pink hue spreads in the sky, the clouds
And the horizon, as the sun sets.

I ask myself: How many more autumn sunsets
Are there left for me and my other half
Before the final sunset of our lives together?

About Postponing

Throughout the years,
I used to write or call my best friend
Quite often.
We both shared, in our background,
World War II and ancestry,
And love for the arts and volunteering.

Once, I let several months pass without calling,
Postponing ...
Postponing ...

And next I heard from an acquaintance
That my dear friend Dalia had died,
Still quite young.

Guilt ridden, I said to myself
No more, no more postponing.

Gifts from Nature

As I walk by a flower garden at noon,
A monarch lands on a Zinnia.
I look at its beautiful wings
And think "How amazing that it can travel
Thousands of miles in its spring migration."
I remember reading of another butterfly,
A painted lady - Vanessa cardui
That travels even farther,
Across the Sahara to Southern Europe.

In the evening, when darkness falls,
I go for another walk,
To breathe some fresh and cooler air.
I see synchronous lighting fireflies
Between the trees, at my eye level.
It is like magic, with flickering lights
On Xmas trees in summer time.

I thank Mother Nature for her generosity
In offering us these gifts
In these difficult times in our lives.

Enjoy What's Left or So Little Time

As daylight fades and stars glitter in the sky
Think of your love of family and friends.

Enjoy your dreams as you travel back in time,
Holding in your arms loves from past and present.

Embrace the time as it races by, and pray
That your prayers may be answered.

♦ ♦ ♦ ♦ ♦

About the Author

Danuta was born in Lithuania. As a young girl during World War II, she lived in Austria as a refugee. After the war, she and her family emigrated to Argentina where she resided for 17 years.

In 1962 upon graduating from medical school at the University of Buenos Aires, she married her lifetime soul mate, Carlos Montorfano, and emigrated to the United States in 1964.

Danuta and Carlos settled in Long Island, New York, where she specialized in Radiology. Throughout her medical career, she taught both residents and medical students, co-authored scientific papers published in medical journals, and she presented scientific exhibits during radiological conferences.

Upon retiring in 2009, Danuta and Carlos moved to Leisure World of Maryland. She enjoys writing poetry about her life experiences and the camaraderie of the Writers Group of Leisure World.

CHAPTER 2

LIFE

By Grace Cooper

Big Little Things

Not diamonds,
Not pearls,
Not huge bank accounts,
No need for these

So welcome,
A smile
A touch,
A call on the phone,
The sound of a voice,

Not the world's riches,
As time moves on,
Most cherished are
Human connections
As we reach the end

Four

One
White
All are good people

Two
Red
Guns and such

Three
Black
Sitting on the street
Hungry in the Tents

Four
Pale
All gone

T'is Of Thee

Across the Mall
Saltine crumbs float
Forgotten pillars of vanquished monuments
Once tall columns blow
In powdered flakes
Clowns parade pathetically
Trying to glue symbols together
Grotesque smiles covering flimsy non documents
Heroes weep
Children scream!
Crumbs drift away in darkness ...

Night

Love crosses darkness
Gently lies beside
Under covers
Never alone

The Day After Tomorrow

Unlost figures
Linger on cave walls,
Earthen jars
Spill out fragile scrolls,
Crumbling words
On disappearing papers
Pencils, quills, pens,
Break into dust,
New words
Preserved?
In the Cloud
Click "print"
The Sun laughs

Misty

Dreams of veiled dress
White satin shoes
Loving caresses
Sweet words of caring
Scattered
Pasted together
Falling apart
Leaving

Refitting
Again
Knives
And roses
Lost beginning
Fake restarts
Bullets and promises
Look ahead
Move on
Ever shrinking horizon
Fade to black

Three A. M.

Reach for a hand
Find a pillow instead
Toss
Turn
Hug the pillow
Toss it on the floor
Fingers grip the sheets
Doze
Pull up the blanket
Turn
Darling
Sweetheart
Turn
A pillow
Move over
Where?
Reach for a hand that isn't there.

Knit One

Sunshine sparkles
Happy children
Run and jump with smiling faces
Purl two
Rain drops patter on the window
Keeping pace with quiet memories
Knit one
Swiftly moves the moon's phases
Purl two
Chalk boards
School books
Plaids and tweeds
Knit one
Pretty dresses
Bow to society
Purl two
Shattered dreams
Patched with tomorrows
Knit one
Help twisted with misunderstandings
Hot sunshine
Thunder showers
Hidden dreams
Hopeless loves
Purl two
Grey with wrinkles
Blue surroundings
Knit one
Purl two

Night Shadows

Every tomorrow never comes,
Every dream is etched on pillows
Every wish is wrapped in hopes
All the words are someone else's
Turn toward stardust
Eyes closed yet more opened
Felt caresses floating on air of midnight
Remembered day echoes
Remembered words
Lying on clouds
Acting as soft touch

Winter Love

Drinking hot cocoa
Wrapped in cozy robes
Watching shows together
Away from howling winds
Legs wrapped lightly around each other
Soft kisses "goodnight"
Soft music
Soft caresses
Away from outside's soft snow
Close and snuggly
"Yes, I love you
Just move over a little
And change the channel
Before you turn out the light."

Facade

Hot steamy shower
Spray of cologne
Silky lingerie
Colorful dress
Bright sunny smile
Cheerful hello
Witty conversation
Sparkly goodbye
Breakable

♦ ♦ ♦ ♦ ♦

About the Author

Grace was born in Washington, DC and lived there during the years of enforced segregation. She learned to read at the age of two and started her writing career at the age of five when one of her poems appeared in her elementary school newspaper. She also wrote and drew cartoon strips for her young friends.

Grace married after graduation from Dunbar High School, the first high school in Washington DC - not just the first high school for the "colored" children as some think. She continued her education, first working and going to school part time, later receiving scholarships for college study as she raised a family of four children. She received the Bachelor of Science in Secondary English Education from the DC Teachers College, the Master of Science in Urban Language from the Federal City College, and Doctor of Philosophy in Psycholinguistics from the Howard University. She took additional graduate work at Georgetown University and received a special faculty grant for study in Biblical studies at Yale University.

Throughout her life, her writing continues. Much of her work life focused on her writing skills. She published many articles and books during her career including: public relations for the C & P Telephone Company, language research for the George Washington University, writer for The Child Welfare League of America, and several teaching positions in English, history, and art, from junior high school through university level.

Twice she received special faculty grants for summer work at the United States Central Intelligence Agency.

After retirement, she continued writing and was a poet for the Takoma Park Senior Citizens program, which featured many of her poems in its newsletter, and presented regular poetry readings for the public. She left the position once she moved to Leisure World in Montgomery County.

Grace was also co-founder of the M Ensemble Company of Miami Florida, for which she wrote articles for The Miami Herald and plays for the company. Upon her return to Washington DC, she wrote and had produced several plays, many for the Howard University Players. Her most widely produced play was a children's play, written for the debut of the Howard University Children's Theater, "Kojo and the Leopard." The play has been performed by schools, universities, and other theater groups around the country and was reviewed in The Washington Star. She has written novels, short stories, and poetry. Writing poetry is her current love.

CHAPTER 3

TALE SPIN

By John Moens

The Cruise

"Good morning, Mr. Johnson. Nice to see you this morning."

"Pardon me, but who are you?"

"I'm Agatha Morley. Call me Aggie. How are we doing today?"

"Well Aggie, I don't know how "we" are doing, but I am in a hospital bed, living with an IV, with nothing to do but watch TV and wait for the doctors to tell me when I am dead. Now, let me try to be a little more clear. Who the Hell is Agatha Morley?"

"Your wife contacted the Travis Agency. They sent me."

"The trip? I'm sorry. I thought you were coming next week."

"Summer is our slow season, so the Agency moved up your appointment. I notified the hospital and assumed they informed you. The fault is mine. You know what they say about the word assume?"

"Oh yes. You make an ass of you and me."

"If you prefer, I can stay with the original appointment."

"No--that's alright. Please stay, Agnes ... Aggie."

"Certainly. I will be happy to. Your wife is on the way over. She said that if it's alright with you, we can start without her."

19

"Oh, it's fine with me. Just tell her I'm alone with a twenty-four-year-old blonde. That will get the lead out."

"Down Tiger. Besides, I'm thirty-six and not blonde, Mr. Johnson."

"Call me Al."

"You selected the Mediterranean, one of our most popular tours. Would you like to look through the brochures again?"

"No thanks. Let's get started."

"Would you like something to drink?"

"There's a pitcher of water on the table."

"Wouldn't you like something more exciting? Maybe a banana daiquiri. And to put you in the mood, one of those tiny umbrellas they serve them with on the cruise ship?"

"You can do that?"

"Yes. I checked with your doctor. I'll have the orderly bring one."

After he returned, we began the tour. "Al, I will be your guide to the Island of Rhodes. It is my favorite island because I was born there. Have you ever been to the Mediterranean before?"

"I was never east of Boston."

"Then lean back, close your eyes and relax in your deck chair. Take a few deep breaths and feel the fresh air seeping into your lungs. The first thing you notice is that the water is sky blue. That is how you know you are in the Mediterranean. In the Atlantic, it is murky green or gray in a storm. But here, it is the bluest of blues."

As Mr. Johnson drifted into a gentle sleep, I told him about my island. I told him about the huge pedestal at the entrance to the harbor, upon which the statue of the giant Colossus once stood, the rose wall, the sun-baked beaches, and the old fortress where the Knights of Saint John desperately fought the Turks, now populated only by meandering deer. I told him many things in the next two hours.

But ... I did not tell him what he had forgotten. That his wife had died seven years ago, or that his grown children were no longer interested in visiting him. Nor did I tell him the truth about our appointment: that the doctor said he would probably not be able to survive the week and needed to see me sooner. Gradually, I drew him back from his trance but he sank back to the pillow. He looked peaceful, content. He never woke. Albert Johnson never travelled east of Boston, but he died on the Island of Rhodes.

A Childhood Memory

As a child, I always respected the elderly. I not only respected them, I also listened attentively to my paternal grandparents' stories of the past, thus spurring my lifelong interest in history. My grandparents reminisced about life in occupied Belgium during World War I.

My maternal grandfather died before I was born, but my maternal grandmother, Pearl Fairall, had researched the family tree and shared our family heritage with me. Amongst the best known members of our family was Winfield Scott, an Army officer who fought in the War of 1812 and commanded the American Army in the Mexican War. General Scott, too old to fight in the Civil War, offered command of the Army of the Potomac to an officer who served under him in the Mexican War. Because it would have meant fighting against citizens of his native Virginia, Robert E. Lee turned it down.

One of my favorite stories was of Grandma Fairall's childhood in the Oklahoma Territory. There was not much left of the Wild West at that time, but what remained was in Oklahoma, New Mexico, and Arizona. The day her family arrived in Oklahoma, a miner was killed in a gunfight.

The Fairall family was well-to-do. They had the first brick house in the territory. One sunny afternoon, Grandma Fairall, then a young girl, was sitting on the porch of the brick house when she had an experience she never forgot. The following is the story she told me.

My Mother and I were sitting on our front porch. She was seated in the rocking chair and I sat on the porch railing. We sat quietly for a time--a half hour, maybe more. Suddenly, she glanced at me and in a very calm voice, ordered, "Pearl. Come over and sit by me." As I was comfortable and not bothering anyone, I did not respond.

21

Mother was not used to being ignored, but she remained calm and in a slightly louder voice repeated, "Pearl. I said, come over and sit by me." I heard her the first time and now it was a test of wills. Wild horses could not drag me from my spot. I did not see her hand move slowly to an object beside her. I most certainly did not see her fingers weave around the object and her palm close tightly on it.

The eerie silence was broken when she suddenly rose to her feet with a large stick in her hand. I was frozen in panic as the stick came crashing down. My initial thought was she missed me. That seemed impossible as I was so fearful I had not moved. How could she miss a sitting duck?

Just then I noticed that she was looking past me. Then, I figured it out. There were three of us on the porch that day: myself, Mother, and the dead rattlesnake she just killed.

There's a Bar in the Woods

Joe Youngblood turned off Interstate 84 and swung onto County Road 244 in Oregon. His wife had stopped asking if this trip was really necessary and drifted off to sleep a half hour ago. It was difficult to explain to any woman, but especially to your wife.

But a man would understand. When you get so old you can't swing a golf club, let alone an axe, you need to find a piece of your youth. You need to remember why God put you on this Earth. Some men were born to push paper, and some men, like Joe Youngblood, were born to cut the trees from which the paper was made.

Joe turned the radio on. Irma liked country but she was asleep, so he turned to hard rock. He couldn't recall what music he listened to at the Bar in the Woods, the Bar at the lumber camp, but he remembered that whatever it was it was loud. "Bar in the Woods" was a pun for "Bear in the Woods." When you stepped out of the Bar and into the solitude, the music stayed with you and you could never be sure whether the headache was from the booze or the music.

The people stayed with you, too. He could still see the faces of Big Blue, Stretch, Harvey, Jim, and Ellie. Uh-oh. Ellie. Best not tell Irma about first meeting Ellie there. Irma would think that the trip had something to do with Ellie, his first wife. Far from it. He never hated Ellie, but it took him five years to realize that he didn't love her. She got the house. He got the pickup truck. Seven years later, he got Irma and never wanted anyone or anything more. She was worth the wait.

The car started to swerve and Irma woke up. "Let me drive," Irma said. She didn't say it as an order. She said it tenderly, careful not to bruise his masculine ego. They switched seats.

"Are you okay?" she asked.

"Never better," he lied.

"Take one of your glycerin tablets." He did and she started the car.

"Are we in Canada yet?"

He smiled and leaned back. He expected Irma to switch the radio to country, but she knew that this was his trip and she wanted him to enjoy the full experience. God gave Joe Youngblood Irma, and God was and is and will always be good.

"How much further?"

"Oh, we're close. I can almost smell the beer."

"How close is close."

"Half an hour tops."

Irma was beginning to suspect they were lost, but as long as they were together, that's all that mattered.

"There it is."

"I don't see anything, Joe."

"The old gravel road. That's where the trucks pulled in to get to the camp."

"Well," thought Irma, "He's right about the road." She was happy for Joe. It was no longer a fool's errand.

"Just follow it past the creek and turn left."

"You doing okay, Joe?"

"Up the creek and left."

"Okay. I heard you the first time."

"Turn the radio off. I think I can hear the music."

"Joe, no one has been here in half a century." She regretted saying anything. Irma flipped off the radio. She listened for the music that wasn't there, as if she sensed that Joe could read her thoughts. They had been together so long, maybe he could.

Joe pointed. "There it is. See, I told you."

"Yes, Joe. I see it. You were right."

"I can't believe it. It hasn't changed a bit. Look at that crowd! Let's go in."

"Joe. It's raining. You'll catch pneumonia."

"There's an umbrella in the trunk. Please, Irma."

"Okay, but you stay put." Irma opened the trunk but couldn't find any umbrella. It wouldn't have mattered anyway. Joe slumped down in his seat and the Bar faded into a blur. Irma stared at what Joe had been looking at and saw only darkness.

The Tie

This story is true: all of it. To be honest, I anticipate many readers will think I imagined it. I am not trying to convince you I have some psychic power. I am not trying to manipulate you into adopting my faith. I am hopeful this story brings the reader a sense of calm about death.

In June 1973, my father, Francis Moens, passed away at the age of 51. It was two years after I had been discharged from the Air Force and I was then attending The Ohio State University. I had a sense my mother would not survive him by more than a year. Nevertheless, her sudden and violent death on Valentine's Day 1974 came as a shock.

My father was definitely not the suit-and-tie type, so I provided my mother my black jacket and tie for his burial. Also, I spit polished my black shoes and, although I have an odd sized foot, they fit him perfectly.

About a week after the funeral, mother wanted to visit the grave, so we took a cab. The visit was peaceful, but a violent storm rolled in on the trip home. The sky turned dark and the force of the wind and the rain nearly drove us off the road. We were wet and tired and ever so grateful to be home. I dried off and went to bed. As I slept soundly, at some point, I started dreaming.

Suddenly, the dream was interrupted. Standing in front of me was my father, exactly as I had last seen him, except missing the tie and his collar was open. The only thing I could say to him was, "But you're dead." He acknowledged me. I was stunned at first, and maybe afraid, and definitely confused. I was aware I had been dreaming, however whatever this was, it was far more vivid than any dream I ever had before or since.

Gradually, I relaxed and we had the kind of discussion two normal, ordinary, live people have. Some of it was confidential, and much of it I have forgotten. I asked him if he had seen God and he said, yes, but the question seemed to make him nervous. After he departed, I went back to sleep. Although I was absolutely convinced I had seen him, when I awoke, I tried to be skeptical. Why would a spirit appear fully dressed? And even if you assume the clothes accompanied the spirit, which seemed highly unlikely, why was the collar open and the tie missing?

I had been thinking about my father constantly since the funeral, so it was perfectly logical my mind had created an image. So, by now, reason and logic prevailed. Nevertheless, I mentioned the incident to my mother. She told me she had seen him, too, that evening. "Daddy was trying to make contact with us." For two of us to see him on the same night seemed evidence this was more than a dream. But what about the missing tie? I definitely saw him wearing it in the coffin.

Mom said, "He hated ties and I did not want him to wear one for eternity. I asked the funeral director to remove it after the viewing."

A Piece of Cake

She went from lie to lie, barely pausing to take a breath. The police officer stopped her car about five miles west of Amarillo. The officer asked to see her license and registration. She responded it was in her purse. Where was her purse? She left it in the dressing room of a store. What store? She didn't remember the name. How come the car is registered to a Mr. Chris Biggs? She stated he was her uncle. What is his phone number? She wrote it down and put it in the purse that she left in the store she couldn't remember. Why didn't she log it into her cell phone? She responded he never answers his phone. Then why did she bother to write it down?

By the time I first saw her, she had a public defender at her side. With an FBI agent on one side and a public defender on the other, that should have at least slowed down the flow of falsehoods. Instead, it seemed to accelerate them. But I had not come 700 miles to recover a car I knew was stolen or to build a case for perjury. I was there to solve a murder and, if possible, to prevent two more. Time was not on my side.

I kept asking about her boyfriend. At first, she denied she had one. But too many people had seen her with him, and at least two verified she had referred to him as her true love. As she explained to me, true love was not the same as saying boyfriend. There was a big difference, although she had difficulty explaining what it was.

Although I did not know true love's name, I did know a young man that matched his description with a young woman that matched her description abandoned a Chevy Impala on a gravel road near Guthrie, Oklahoma. They then hiked to a roadside cafe.

At the cafe, they met an elderly couple who agreed to give them a lift. The owner of the cafe thought it was strange the young man was wearing a Rolex watch and dirty t-shirt. Whether for this reason or because the young couple didn't pay for their lunch, the owner called the police and gave the license number of the Buick they drove off in. That turned out to be the car stopped outside Amarillo.

My interest was in the Chevy Impala with the Nebraska plates. The owner was found lying in a ditch near North Platte. I knew I could keep asking questions and hope that after another three hours she would exhaust her supply of lies. That seemed unlikely. There was a possibility that the Biggs were still alive but time was running out. Up until now, the suspect was in control. She knew the facts. I did not. Now I decided to take a chance.

"I think you and your boyfriend murdered the elderly couple. I plan to charge you with first degree murder."

I anticipated the public defender might raise an obstacle, such as where is my evidence, however she had totally ignored him for three hours. Why would she bother listening to him now?

"You don't know anything!" she blurted out. "I tried to save them."

"You tried," I repeated. "Past tense?"

She paused for nearly a full minute, then she nodded. The cat was now out of the bag, but she felt relief that the game was over at last.

"Jerry wanted to shoot them."

"Jerry. Is that the boyfriend?"

"Yes. My fiancée."

"Did Jerry kill the owner of the car with the Nebraska plates?"

She nodded as she said, "Yes."

"Did he kill the elderly couple?"

"Do you want to tell this story or do you want me to?"

"I want you to tell it, in your own words. Please."

For the first time, the suspect gave her real name - Betty. Even now, she refused to give her real last name. She knew all we had to do was check her fingerprints, but it gave her some comfort to know she was, however briefly, still anonymous.

In brief, the story was that the elderly couple had offered them a lift to Phoenix. Jerry planned to kill the couple and drive their car to Mexico. Betty had seen Jerry commit one murder and had no desire to become involved in two more. Every time they were out of earshot of the couple, they argued about it.

The elderly couple could not have been nicer. Mr. Biggs offered to help get Jerry a job with a friend of his who managed a shoe store. Betty was nearly moved to tears when Mrs. Biggs talked about how her husband had lost his job after 35 years when the company went bankrupt. The couple did not have much, however, Mrs. Biggs added, "We have each other."

That night, Betty told Jerry that if he didn't give her the gun, she would call off their engagement. Whatever Jerry's faults, he did love Betty, even more than he loved killing people. He gave her the gun.

"So, are the Biggs still alive?" I asked.

"She shook her head and, this time, several minutes passed before she was able to utter the word "No." "We pulled off the road and Mr. Biggs found this beautiful spot where we could spend the night. Jerry liked it because it was secluded and we would not be visible from the highway."

"Cindy, that is Mrs. Biggs, said there would be no need to go to the expense of a diner and a motel. In the car, there were baskets of food, water, tissue, toiletries, and some sleeping bags. They lived in their car, so they thought of everything. The food was great. All of it home cooked, although it never occurred to me to ask in whose home they cooked it or when. So, we ate and slept under the stars.

"About 2 a.m., Jerry woke up. He was not feeling well, so I called Cindy. She gave him some medicine and suggested he lie down. Then she asked me how I was doing. I told her, "I felt fine." Since we ate the same food, the problem didn't seem to have anything to do with the dinner.

"Shortly before dawn, I heard voices. Jerry managed to fall back to sleep, but I was so worried about him, I could not. I heard Cindy say, 'Be sure and get his watch.' I pretended to be asleep but I could see he was carrying a shovel. Mr. Biggs put it down as he removed Jerry's watch. Then he began digging a grave. Just then, I sat up and Mr. Biggs reacted like he had seen a ghost. Cindy yelled for him to hit me with the shovel. Then I shot them."

"Both of them?" I asked.

"Both," Betty responded.

With Betty's help, we located the car and found the bodies. The fingerprints on the gun matched Jerry's and Betty's. Therefore, it was possible Betty's story was just that, a story. I got the autopsy report on the three bodies and discussed it with Betty.

"The picnic food you ate?"

"Yes?"

"Did you both eat exactly the same thing?"

"Yes. The same."

"What about desert?"

"Desert?"

"The homemade German chocolate cake."

"Oh. I gave him my piece. I'm diabetic."

"That's why you're alive."

C not K

Simon O'Toole saw his grandmother for the last time on January 1, 1901, the first day of the first month of the new century. From her deathbed, Ida Claiborne O'Toole vowed she would watch over eight-year-old Simon all the days of his life.

Six years later, the coal companies were hiring men to work in the mines. Fourteen-year-old Simon stepped forward, but the foreman laughed at him. Simon boasted he would bring out more coal than any man that day, so the foreman hired him. When the mine owner questioned the foreman, he explained he agreed to take Simon for his spunk, and to teach him a lesson, he had no intention of paying him. Just before noon, a section of the mine collapsed. Of the entire crew, the rescuers found only Simon alive, clinging to a lump of coal. It was the only coal to come out of the mine that day. Simon believed it was his grandmother watching over him, but more than one man thought it might be the devil. Afterwards, Simon was able to find enough work to provide all necessities, but he never worked in the mines again.

One day, nineteen-year-old Simon found his fortune laying in a Southampton street: a steamship ticket for America. He ran all the way to the pub where his sweetheart's father, Mr. Wendell Graham worked and informed him of the good news. He asked Mr. Graham's permission to marry his daughter, Katie, and take her with him.

"Do you have money for another ticket, or do you plan for her to swim alongside?"

Simon proposed they play a single hand of poker, with the ticket as stakes. If Simon won, Mr. Graham would pay for another ticket. Mr. Graham said, "Okay. Welsh luck against the luck of the Irish. Let's have at it, and may the better man win."

Katie arrived in time to see Simon lay down a pair of kings and a pair of aces. Her father gave him the money. Simon then asked to see his cards. "You will not be embarrassing me, Lad. Off with you, and don't expect any handouts from me when your luck runs out.

Mr. Graham was a strong man but not strong enough to break his daughter's heart by revealing his hand: Ace, King, Queen, Jack and 10 of clubs. Only love could beat a straight flush. Mr. Graham fought to hold back his tears as he bid Katie farewell.

Simon purchased another ticket and, with Katie clutching his arm, proceeded up the gang plank. Proudly, he handed the two tickets to the Bursar. He nodded and smiled, welcoming them. He glanced at Katie's ticket and handed it back. Then he carefully studied Simon's ticket. He showed the ticket to the Bobby standing beside him and the Bobby nodded.

"Son," stated the Bobby, "this ticket is counterfeit. You'll have to come with me."

And that's where Simon O'Toole's journey to America ended. As he stood at the dock, he observed the great liner pull away. Then there was one brief glimmer of hope. An American liner pulled loose from its moorings and nearly collided with the British ship. In his mind, Simon imagined the British liner returning to its dock, and the Bobby apologizing for mistaking a perfectly good ticket. Grandmother was still watching over him. But with his eyes, he saw the liner proceed out to sea and the Bobby holding his ticket and his arm.

The Bobby took Simon to the pub with Katie crying and clinging to his arm. The Bobby informed Mr. Graham, "This rascal says you can vouch for him. He has a counterfeit ticket."

"He is no criminal," Mr. Graham replied, "just Irish."

Mr. Graham was so happy to get his daughter back, he hired Simon to work in the pub. Simon was disappointed that he would never see

America. His grandmother had watched over him up until now, so he forgave her for this one time. Simon wondered how the Bobby knew the ticket was counterfeit, so he showed it once again to Mr. Graham.

"There's your answer Lad. You spell Titanic with a *c* not a *k*."

The Christmas Tree

In December 1944, it looked like the German army was on the verge of collapse. Allied armies were on the offensive everywhere and the Royal Air Force and U.S. Army Air Force dominated the skies. But the Germans secretly moved in fresh, battle-hardened troops and armor from the Eastern front. The counterattack, which became known as the Battle of the Bulge, fell on green troops who were routed. The attack gradually bogged down as veteran units blocked the advance at road junctions, the most famous was the stand of the 101st parachute regiment at Bastogne, Belgium. But there was fighting in hundreds of locations, many of which did not even have a name.

One such nameless place was a clump of trees that, for all we knew might have been in Luxembourg, and for all we cared, could have been in Hooterville. There gathered the shattered and demoralized remnants of several companies. These refugees included everything from infantry to military police to supply clerks. We were not fighting to defend anything from the Germans and not worth their attention. Every now and then, an artillery shell would burst in our area. There were so few of us left that nine out of ten times, it tore up trees and dirt and melted some snow without hitting anyone. The tenth time, however ... well, when your time comes, it comes.

Fortunately, for us, we were not the intended target. No one but us was aware anyone was there. The shells were intended for significant targets further away, but cold artillery tends to fire short. Every now and then, we would radio for help but we always got Christmas music in return. It was not some effort to build up Allied morale. The damn Germans were messing with our communications by broadcasting Christmas carols night and day.

With all you read about the tactics and strategy of the Bulge, I can tell you for our part it can be summed up in five C's: casualties, chaos,

Christmas Carols, C rations, and COLD. It's not by accident I put cold in all capitals. If someone remembers it differently, feel free to tell me, "You've lost your marbles, Joe."

Two days before Christmas, we hear some noise on our left flank. It is either wildlife, retreating Americans, or the advancing Germans. There's a shot. (You know how they always say, "Shots ring out?" I never heard a shot ring in my life.) It breaks the silence and, to us, it sounds like a cannon went off. We don't know whether it's a German, or one of our guys panicked, or a retreating American mistook us for Germans, but we can now rule out wildlife.

Then there was stillness. It is almost certainly a German, trying to draw our fire. We do not respond. The Germans don't know if anyone is here, but they are cautious. Two or three of them move from the cover of the trees, and we can be certain there are more behind them in the trees covering them. Now, there's no longer any point in hiding our presence.

Every German who stepped forward is mowed down. Then the troops behind them opened up on us and we focused all our fire on them. That was a mistake. We had no idea how many people were in the trees, but at least a hundred were sneaking up behind us. They hit us by surprise.

Had they not been right on top of us, we might have surrendered, but they weren't taking prisoners. The fighting became hand-to-hand. They had the better strategy and the better tactics, and since we were green, almost certainly the better soldiers. Faced with no other option than to fight or die, we fought better than we were. It was enough, just barely enough, to stop them. They retreated.

They probably figured it wasn't worth the delay or casualties to continue the fight when artillery could blow us to bits in less than a half hour. Nevertheless, we were exhilarated to finally win something. No one was more excited than PFC Roy Czolgosz, and he is what this story is all about. Or rather, his tree is what this story is all about.

A grenade had gone off near his foxhole and the tree was loaded with shrapnel. It was shattered and ugly, but to Czolgosz, it was the most beautiful tree he ever met. In his view, the tree had given its life for him, which may sound absolutely nuts but it happens to be true. And Czolgosz was an honorable man. He was indebted to that tree and the tree, although wounded, was a living thing and an innocent victim.

As we were all going to die or be captured anyway, no one would have cared if he married the tree. Roy didn't go that far, but I can honestly say, as of that day, I have seen everything. He decided that everybody was going to show the tree proper respect. He began by gathering empty c-ration cans. We had more of them than ammo. He also removed the laces from the boots of dead Germans. They would not miss them. Then, he borrowed a pair of wire cutters. You would think that someone would have said something to him, but we were so exhausted and morale was so low that we just ignored him.

The someone who may have said something was Lieutenant Gregg, the only surviving officer, but Gregg had his hands full. We had more dead than living, and more wounded than fit. We were down to only seventeen men who were in fighting shape and even half of those were walking wounded. And in my count, I am not including the Lieutenant. There was not a mark on him, but his mind was gone.

So Czolgosz carried on and, by dawn, we saw the results of his work. He had cut and molded the metal from the ration cans into little stars and used the shoestrings to hang the stars from his tree. Anywhere else, folks would have called it pathetic and recommended him for a Section 8, but here, we called it Christmas. We all expected it to be our last. We were all out of stuff to treat the wounded, and there was no corpsman to help them. Constant moaning all the time gradually grew fainter as more men died.

Someone mentioned Roy's tree to one of the wounded and he asked to look at it. So we laid his stretcher beside it. As it seemed to have a calming effect on him, we laid two more stretchers beside it. One man was puzzled, but the other thought about home. We told the wounded they would be going home soon as the army was counter attacking and the Germans were on the run. If you really don't know whether it's true or not, is it a lie? We sang a few Christmas carols, but one guy was angry because it reminded him of what the Germans were doing to our communications. So the caroling was brief.

All in all, what we expected to be our last day on Earth began well. Then Czolgosz noticed something moving in the woods. If they could have waited just one more day we would have lived 'til Christmas. It was a German soldier with a white flag. This was totally unexpected. We were expecting the German artillery to blow us to bits. We let him come closer. He announced that his Captain was giving us permission to surrender. No kidding. He didn't say "asking" or "demanding."

The Germans were cutting us a break. Turn down the offer and we were dead. So what did we do? Tell them Americans don't surrender? Negotiate terms? Tell them "nuts" like McAuliffe did at Bastogne? We had heard that Americans were being murdered after surrendering, so we had reservations. But if the only options are die if you don't or maybe die if you do, the word "maybe" sounds sweet.

The German soldiers came forward. Several of us could speak some German but we pretended we couldn't. It didn't matter. The Germans didn't care whether we could understand them or not. They were in charge. Some of what I'm about to say I didn't learn until much later, but in the interest of keeping it short, here is what happened. When they realized the Lieutenant was nuts, the Captain met with Sergeant Crisp. The Captain had served on the Eastern front and murdered more than a few Russian prisoners. Still, he had a different attitude towards Christians.

He asked Crispy if there were any Jews among us. We didn't know, but Crisp said no. While the German offensive was sputtering out and the Captain had no qualms about killing us if we were slowing him down, he figured the Americans may not take vengeance if they knew Allied prisoners were being treated humanely.

Next something happened that almost blew the whole deal. The Captain looked at the bodies of German soldiers. He asked why they hadn't been buried. Crisp explained we were so few that we didn't even have the manpower to bury our own dead. We had to care for the wounded and prepare for a counterattack. The Captain appeared satisfied with the answer, but then, he noticed the laces missing from the boots of the dead Germans. He didn't understand it, but put two and two together and got five.

"He thinks you are robbing the dead," explained his aide.

Realizing the Captain might call the whole thing off, Crispy told them we took only the laces and their weapons. When the aide asked him why, Crisp took them to see the tree. The Captain was puzzled. He laughed at first, but lapsed into silence. You could tell by looking at him, the Captain was no longer here. Where he was and what he was thinking, no one knows but him. No one spoke to him.

Several minutes passed before he returned to the real world. After that, we started walking towards captivity. For us, the war was over. Most of us survived past VE Day, and a few did not. After the war, I often think about the friends I lost. Once in a while, I think about that tree. I once dreamed of finding it standing big and tall, dwarfing the little rusted stars that may have somehow survived three quarters of a century. And a child asking, how did the tiny pieces of metal get way up there? More than likely, the tree died long ago, but one can dream.

Rain Washes Everything Clean

The song says West Virginia is "Almost Heaven," but as I recall, it was pure Hell that dark night. Rainwater burst down the mountainsides, battering trees, molesting cabins, flooding all the abandoned mines, and sweeping the unsheltered--which fortunately, was few--into the valleys below.

If that wasn't bad enough, (and believe me, it WAS bad enough) the rain turned to sleet in the morning and hail by the next evening. That being said, we were fortunate. There had been plenty of warning and, while you could always count on the occasional fool attempting to drive through the abyss, the fools were mostly sleeping that night.

All things considered, Monongalia County's death toll of five was a near miracle. I refrain from saying "only five." Each life snuffed out meant something to someone, and quite possibly, meant everything to someone.

As a deputy sheriff in Morgantown, I have seen more than one dead body. You see how vicious human beings can be to each other. Perhaps no better example of this was the notorious Skylar Neese case. Skylar was a bright 16-year-old who lived over at Star City, just south of us. She was murdered in Pennsylvania by two teenage girls. Ms. Neese was stabbed more than 50 times. When asked why, one of the girls explained, "We just didn't like her anymore."

If you watch detective shows on TV, "motive" seems to be as good as fingerprints. The super sleuth deduces Joe Jones HAD to be the murderer because he HAD the motive. Do you think a jury is going to understand two people joined in a murder simply because they stopped liking someone? That's one reason you have to be very careful what you say in an interrogation. If you suggest a possible motive, the suspect may simply agree with you rather than admit he is too stupid to have one. Every now and then, I ask myself, if I can deal with all this, is it possible that I'm a little nuts, too?

You might assume that when it is a natural disaster instead of a murder, it's not so bad. No psychos to deal with and no drunks. But even with natural causes, you still have to inform the family that their son, their daughter, their spouse, their parent has died.

Then you stand there and watch their world collapse.

The Mon (what natives call the Monongahela River) does not care where it dumps the bodies, so we got calls all day long from worried relatives. We were surprised several of them came from our northern neighbor, Pennsylvania. If your knowledge of the Mon is based solely on glancing at the map, that doesn't strike you as strange. The Mon is 130 miles long and Pennsylvania is a stone's throw from Morgantown, West Virginia, (granted you will need a pretty good arm) where the sheriff's office is located. But--and this is an important but--the Monongahela River is one of the few rivers in the United States that flows northward. So to get to us, bodies would have to swim against the current.

A total of five bodies were found in the next two weeks. None of them were found in our jurisdiction. A few weeks after that, I took a couple days off to relax at home. I live out in the woods, about one hour's drive from Morgantown. Six months ago, almost to the day, I married Crystal. Crystal is a city girl, born and raised in Philadelphia.

When she first saw where I live, she was surprised it was a regular house and not a cabin. I told her that regardless of what she may have heard, we are very civilized out here: we have flush toilets and, when our kerosene lamps don't work, we flick on the light switch.

We also have Wilbur, Orville, and Rainy running about the house. They are my three hunting dogs. I was a Security cop when I was in the Air Force, which is how I came up with Wilbur and Orville. Since there were only two Wright brothers, I named Rainy after the weather the day I picked him up from the shelter. Crystal is afraid of hunting dogs, and dogs can sense that. But she oozes kindness and the dogs came to love her anyway.

Wilbur is pretty old and messed up the car one day. After that, I couldn't keep him in the house and I wouldn't have him put to sleep. So, I built him a dog house. It gets awfully cold outside, so I lined it with bricks. Here is the best part. I rigged it with a heating system. That dog lives high on the hog in his retirement.

People who love dogs probably do not need an explanation why I went to all this trouble, but Wilbur is a special dog. Back when I just had Wilbur and Orville. I stepped off the path one snowy day and went plunging into the water. Orville just stood there barking his fool head off. Wilbur immediately jumped into the water. As you have probably guessed, this resulted in a dramatic rescue. Wilbur did not understand how cold the water could be and started to go under. Fortunately, I had fallen into a big hole rather than a creek. I hauled Wilbur's ass and mine out of the water and took us home. I looked at him and asked, "Who did you think you were, Lassie?" However, I knew that I had a dog that would die for me.

One morning at breakfast, Crystal reminded me I received a phone message from my Pa. Yeah, I knew it. He rarely calls me and I even more rarely return his calls.

"What's between you and your Dad?"

"Nothing. And that's the way I intend to keep it."

"Honey, it isn't right. He's all the family you've got."

"No, you're all the family I have. You and the pack." (By pack, I meant the dogs.)

"I don't want something weighing on your heart all the time."

We finished breakfast in silence. About half an hour later, my cell phone rang. I thought to myself, "Why couldn't it have rung a half an hour earlier." It was the sheriff. He informed me that two hikers had found a body wedged in the rocks along the river bank less than ten miles from where I live. He apologized for interrupting a day off but promised to make it up to me.

The body was that of a young woman, say 20 to 25. Jane Doe was badly battered, quite possibly while being thrust against rocks by the raging river during the flood. The body was in an area that has been previously searched, so it might have been missed. But that was not the only possibility.

I did not merely assume that this was a sixth victim of the flood, but there were other clues. The wounds did not look fresh. This could mean that the body came to a rest somewhere else and the wind or a change in direction of the current pried it loose and moved it along. The body could also have been submerged and risen to the surface. Yet another possibility was that a person had dumped it here.

Her teeth were in really bad shape, and not just from the battering. The dental work was minimal and no attempt at cosmetic dentistry. Whoever she was, she had lived a hard life. Maybe whatever she did not get in this world, she would get in the next.

Although some consider it a waste of time, we searched thoroughly for a purse but found nothing. No footprints or tire tracks on either river bank. The County Coroner determined that she died by drowning. Everything seemed to say she was a flood victim. Victim number six was not substantially different from victims one through five.

Everything? Well, almost everything. None of the other five were wearing expensive jewelry. A gold bracelet had managed to remain clasped to her mangled wrist. This seemed to rule out that she was beaten and robbed. Noting the poor condition of her teeth, it seemed unlikely the bracelet belonged to her. Another thing was no one had inquired about victim number six. No one. That would suggest she was a tourist or just passing through or she lived alone.

To go any further, we needed some help. It began with calling other jurisdictions. We also called in a sketch artist, although she didn't have much to work with. Eventually, we went to the news media. It was on a Thursday that Molly, our Secretary told me a Mr. Hurley Jones was here to see me.

I can only describe him this way: if you have ever seen an old photo of "Devil Anse" Hatfield of the Hatfield and McCoy feud, this is his twin. Hurley was "hill people" and didn't need any ID to prove it. So I don't give the wrong impression, he was polite, you might even say noble in a way. He looked you in the eye and you sensed he was leveling with you. His hair was long and he had a beard, but he wore a jacket and tie. His shoes were old but he shined them. All of this said to me, I'm in your world now and I will respect that.

"How can I help you, Mr. Jones?"

"Call me, Hurl. Everybody does."

"Okay, Hurl. My name's George."

We shook hands. "Nice to meet you, George. I'm here for two reasons. Number one, is to see my daughter. If it's her, I will give you reason number two."

"Do you think the woman we've found is your daughter?"

"If she's wearing a gold bracelet, she is." We hadn't mentioned the gold bracelet. So far, so good. I put on a pair of gloves, went to the safe, and pulled out an evidence bag. From the bag, I extracted the bracelet.

"That's it," Hurley said. "You can keep the bracelet. It ain't mine and it ain't hers."

"We can't do that, Hurl."

"Why not?"

"It's not ours."

"Don't that beat all? Two women died for it and now, nobody wants it?"

"Sir. You have something to tell me; something that will help me clear up all this. I can't do it without your help. Please do."

He sat there, staring straight ahead for several minutes. Then he started to pray. Then he looked at me as if he had just remembered I was in the room.

"I am here to turn myself in. Chrissy is my daughter. I killed her. That's not why I am turning myself in. No court on Earth can convict me for Chrissy, but it's what happened after."

"Hurl, I don't know what this is all about but I have the duty to inform you that you have the right to remain silent and anything you say may be used against you in a court of law. You have the right to the presence of an attorney before questioning can begin. If you cannot afford one, one will be appointed for you. Do you understand all this?"

He nodded.

I then informed him I was going to tape record our conversation. I also asked Deputy Gibson to join us. Hurl declined an attorney. As it turned out, it wasn't much of a conversation. He did nearly all the talking. He gave me his name and daughter's name and informed me he lived in a cabin six miles from Tygart. The rest of this is from the transcript.

"Last year, Chrissy, my daughter, came into my room and showed me a new bracelet she was wearing. She told me a nice rich lady gave it to her. Chrissy's mother, bless her soul, raised her as a Baptist. But she can lie like a rug and then some. I told Chrissy I may not have a college education, but rich ladies do not give mountain folk expensive bracelets, especially if they are nice rich ladies. It took half the night but I got the truth of the matter. Chrissy never had anything pretty. She wanted that gold bracelet enough to ... well, to kill for it. That's just what she done.

"She said it just started out as an ordinary day. Out of nowhere comes this lady all dressed up. Well, I guess rich folks wouldn't call it dressed up ... they would call it casual. Wearing those jeans that you pay extra to rip holes in them. I tell you, people with money are plum crazy. She was walking around in the woods "hiking" and managed to get lost. Stands there holding a map and a compass and doesn't have a clue where she is. Chrissy points her the way to Palatine, then she noticed the nice bracelet. First, Chrissy asks if she can have it. Chrissy didn't think anyone would parade around with a real gold bracelet where everybody can see it. Then she tries to take it. The lady screams and Chrissy knows she's in trouble. Well, one thing leads to another and suddenly Chrissy finds her hunting knife in her hand.

"She showed me where she buried the body. We dug it up.

"The rich lady had a driver's license. Her name was Eleanor Ford. I made her a decent coffin, best I ever made. I could not risk making a marker, cause someone might spot it and start asking questions. But I buried her near an old elm tree to be able to find the grave if I needed to. The flood leaked into the coffin and I cleaned it out.

"I told Chrissy I wouldn't turn her in but she was no longer welcome in my home. I gave her a tent and blankets. She knew how to make a fire without burning down the woods. Once, it got so cold she nearly died and I let up. I let her stay in the house, then back out she went when it warmed a bit. It was not I was so mad at her. I just wanted her to see reason and turn herself in. She said she would do it only if they let her keep the bracelet.

"Then the rains came and swept her away. I ask your permission for me to make my daughter a coffin and bury her. Then you can do what you want with me. That's it. I hope Miss Ford's family can ever forgive Chrissy and me, though neither one of us deserve it.

As I listened to all this, I thought of my relationship with my own father. All my life, I wanted my father's respect. He had been a police officer. When I went into the Air Force, he never wrote me. When I came out, I moved to West Virginia and became a deputy. I thought, at last he would notice I admired him and ... well, I needed him. I drove all the way to Richmond to let him see me in my new deputy's uniform. He just glanced at my black and gray deputy's uniform with the badge and said, "This is the big surprise?" Then he went in the kitchen and got a beer. That was it. All I could say was goodbye, at least, I think I said goodbye.

And right now, I was facing a man who sacrificed everything for his daughter: his honor, his dignity, his pride, and quite possibly his freedom. Although I respected Hurl, even felt sympathy towards him, he was not the victim. I had to balance this against what Miss Ford's family had suffered. Actually, it turned out to be Mrs. Ford (she was separated and had one daughter). They had gone for nearly a year without knowing what had happened to her. Hurl had hidden the body and had withheld evidence. His actions, regardless of his good intentions, had led to his daughter's death. His knowing that would be a greater burden than any court could impose. Although the final decision must be in the hands of a jury. It would be my job to testify at his trial. I did my job.

There isn't much I can add. The Ford family was devastated, but her sister, Ellen, attended the funeral when Hurl buried his daughter and invited him to attend the funeral when Eleanor Ford was buried again. The judge granted parole to Hurl and Hurl thanked him.

Molly, our secretary, has a friend in Palatine who graciously agreed to check up on Hurl every now and then to make sure he is alright. Oh, yes: the gold bracelet. Eleanor's daughter is grown and she has it. I don't know if the family ever told her the story behind it.

♦ ♦ ♦ ♦ ♦

About the Author

John Moens was born in New York City during the "baby boom." He graduated from The Ohio State University with a B.S. degree in Social Science. After serving in the United States Air Force, John taught high school for one year in Columbus, Ohio. In 1973, he entered the Civil Service retiring in 2011 as an Industry Specialist for the Energy Information Administration. Among his favorite authors are Elmore Leonard, Edgar Alan Poe, Ambrose Bierce, and O. Henry. He has been writing short stories as a hobby since elementary school.

CHAPTER 4

LIFETIME MEMORIES

By Jerry Udell

Riverside Amusement Park

The Riverside Amusement Park was a giant park located in central Indianapolis and featured the full complement of carnival rides and games and perhaps as many as 10 to 12 baseball diamonds. My high school baseball team, Shortridge, played many of its games in this park. The diamonds were laid out on widely different levels.

On one particular afternoon, we were playing on the most highly elevated playing field in the sports complex. The field we were playing barely contained the infield before dropping, parallel aside the first base line, many, many yards on a steep incline down to the adjacent baseball diamond.

I was a right-handed batter. I swung late on a pitch and hit the ball on the extreme end of the bat. The ball, wildly rotating, cleared the first baseman's head by about four feet. You could hear the ball make a weird spinning sound as it sailed over his outstretched hand. The ball barely stayed fair, but then bounced a hard right straight down the giant hill on which our diamond was located.

It ended up on the lower playing field, rolling towards a startled short stop, who was, as he should have been, focused on the batter at home plate on his field. But there came my ball, trickling down the gigantic hill toward his right foot.

43

If that was not confusing enough, he then noticed the catcher, in full protective gear, the pitcher, and first baseman from the team we were opposing, racing down the hill from our elevated diamond to set up some kind of relay to get my ball up on our diamond to stop my running the bases.

Meanwhile, I nearly "succumbed" while rounding second base and heading for third base. (At 5'10" and 150 pounds, I didn't have much practice running out home runs!)

As my ball was gradually being relayed up to our playing field, I couldn't run much farther. Finally, my right foot hit HOME PLATE! The umpire yelled, "Safe!" and I then collapsed into the arms of my congratulating teammates - many were hysterically laughing. I had just hit the most bizarre, funkiest home run in Shortridge history!

Broad Ripple

In the 1950's, the Broad Ripple section of Indianapolis was on the way to becoming a quaint, artsy, "in place" extension of Indianapolis. But to most of us, it was just the home of our northside school rival. We knew a few kids from their school, but in general there wasn't that much interaction between students.

It wasn't until I entered Hanover College and was having trouble with freshman Biology when I met an attractive Broad Ripple co-ed who happened to be a straight A student. I asked if she would tutor me for our midterm. She agreed. We discovered we lived on adjacent streets in Indianapolis - but 17 blocks apart.

She got her A in biology. I got through. Mission accomplished!

We decided to date that summer. I asked her if she liked bowling. She said "Yes." When I picked her up and met her Mom and Dad, I noticed a living room bookcase full of bowling trophies. I asked her if they were her Dad's. She modestly replied, "No, they're mine."

She trounced me on the lanes that night but, I did not "strikeout." She ultimately became my wife, and our 61-year romance continues to this day.

Tribute to My Dad: Fall 1956

Three years ago, I lost my father. He was 101! During our 76 years together, he passed his love of country and interest in sports on to me, his only child.

One day in the fall of 1956, he asked, "Jer, how'd you like to go to New York with me on a business trip?" Obviously, my response was, "Dad that would be great!"

By way of background, I was born and raised in Indiana at a time when there was very little theater in Indianapolis and no professional sports teams within the state. We only had summer stock featuring a few Broadway plays from the 30s and 40s and no professional sports franchises. The Hoosier State with Indiana and Purdue Universities and, of course, Notre Dame was a bustling hub for college football, not professional sports.

As a result, I had never personally seen a professional game or a Broadway play. As the day of our departure neared, Dad said "Son, I have tickets to some events in New York that I think we'll enjoy."

We saw "My Fair Lady" and a dramatic play called "Raisin in the Sun," starring the young unknown African American actor named Sidney Poitier, (who eight years later would be the first of his race to win the Best Actor Academy Award) AND ... tickets to three World Series games featuring the Yankees versus the Dodgers. (It was to be the last Subway Series as the Dodgers moved to Los Angeles, the next year.)

The Broadway plays left a lasting impression on me. My wife and I currently usher in three Montgomery County theaters. But the event that imprints the trip in my mind revolves around the World Series.

We saw two Series games played in the week we arrived and had tickets for Monday's game in Yankee Stadium. As my Dad was aware I had a major event scheduled in High School, he gave me the choice of going home on Sunday or staying to watch the game on Monday.

I was one of the two finalists running for Junior Class President and the one and only opportunity for campaign speeches were to be given by me and my opponent at 10:00 Monday morning!

Our Shortridge High School was one of the oldest in Indiana with 3,000 students and had some very conservative traditional rules, one of which was there were only two sets of class officers - Junior and Senior. So, this was a big deal for me. I said, "Dad, I don't think they will vote for me if I am not even there!" He agreed and we sold our tickets to the game and headed back to Indianapolis.

On Monday morning, the speeches took place as scheduled. They were predictably mundane and forgettable. At 3:30 that afternoon my locker mate Elliott Nelson came up to me and said 14 of the most memorable words anyone has said to me in my life. "Have you heard what Don Larsen (the starting pitcher for the Yankees) got going in the bottom of the 7th?"

October 8, 1956, Don Larson, a mediocre pitcher (as confirmed by his lifetime record of 81 wins and 91 losses) pitched the only no-hit, no-run complete game in World Series history - without the Udells in attendance!

Thirty years later, I was in Cooperstown, New York on a business trip. I walked past a baseball souvenir shop when, out of the corner of my eye, I saw a picture of Don Larson and an autographed ball for sale! I decided on the spot I'd pay up to $200 for it. I walked in the shop with my hand on my wallet and nervously asked the clerk, "How much for the Larsen ball?" He replied, "$35" You never saw $35 come out of a wallet any faster!

Two months later on Christmas morning, I handed my Dad two presents - one was a plastic baseball stand and the other a baseball signed "Don Larson, October 8, 1956."

And, oh, by the way, YES, I was elected Junior Class President!

Mom and Me

My mother died several years ago at the age of 88. She did not go to college. Mom's major calling was of a housewife. She kept a beautiful home and was quite an accomplished, self-trained interior decorator. I remember our house being totally redone three or four times. Our home and tending to the needs of her husband and raising her only child was the major focus in life. She would occasionally volunteer for causes that interested her.

One volunteer organization was a group of women dedicated to lowering the high school dropout rate in Indianapolis. Its work was the subject of a nice article in the Indianapolis star. I was working as an intern (my first post college job) for Senator Birch Bayh (D-IND). I called the article to his attention. He inserted it into the congressional record as a tribute to the group. My Mom's name in the congressional record! Pretty neat!

In the '70s and '80s, there were a great number of books written by people who experienced "after-death" experiences and returned to life after serious accidents or major operations. They were able to recount in great detail the location of objects in the operating room, things that were done and said during surgery, etc. The books were short, mostly paperbacks, and made fascinating reading.

One day, while I was describing these books to my mother, many of which involved women in childbirth. My mother's face fell, and her eyes widened. She teared up and said, "Jerry, that's what happened to me when you were born!"

She related to me that my birth was difficult - a fact I had known all my life. That is why I was an only child. Having another was too dangerous.

Mom related a difficult, painful, and lengthy birthing process. She recalled being whisked at great speed down a dark tunnel arriving at the end of the tunnel at a bright light that was peaceful, warm, and alluring and being told she could enter the light or turn back. She communicated with the spirit she wanted "to go back and raise her son." By this time, Mom and I were sobbing, laughing, and hugging all at once.

Although the phenomenon of after-death experiences has been the subject matter of books, television shows, and investigations since Mom and I had our talk, there is no consensus among the medical or spiritual communities as to the origins of these incidents and their meaning. But Mom and I have a pretty good idea as to what it meant to us. This is where our strong bond began!

The Big Red Airplane

I attended Public School 66 in Indianapolis. I walked to school in the morning, home for lunch, and back for the afternoon session. Most of the bookcases in our classrooms, as many throughout Indianapolis, were built by the Udell Woodenware Works, a prominent Hoosier business founded in 1870 by a distant relative of our family.

My memories of grade school are fading as I am in the midst of my 81st year. But one day remains burned in my memory. It remains so because it involves my personal behavior so uncharacteristic I cannot ever remember doing anything in my life nearly so outrageous.

I believe most people whose paths I have crossed would agree I am even tempered. But this one day I just plain "lost it!" I have no idea what grade I was in or how old I was, but crayons were still a part of our mandatory educational toolbox.

Dick Sunman was a friend and sat right next to me. He was a cute small kid with a blond crew cut, but his concentration skills would have today been of concern to his parents and teachers. Put bluntly, he had none.

Miss Pauline Hammer was our teacher. Her title "Miss" hinted at a touch of loneliness. Her last name - Hammer - could not have been more appropriate. She was as tough as nails and ran a tight ship.

During the day in question, Miss Hammer started the lesson by explaining a mathematical process by which one used to solve the problems presented on the front page of our worksheet. She then told us to tackle our worksheet.

Dick, who had been visiting his "other universe," suddenly realized he hadn't been listening to Miss Hammer. As he did every day, he turned to me and asked, "What are we supposed to do now?" Every day it was the same. He always asked me what to do. Without any premeditation or forethought, I looked Dick straight in the eye and said, "She said to turn your paper over and draw a big red airplane."

Incredulously, Dick said, "What??"

And I replied with total sincerity, "Draw a big red airplane on the back of your math paper and make it as red as you can."

Dick flipped his paper over and began drawing a 'big red airplane.' He was pushing his red crayon so hard; it was flaking off into little red pieces. Dick's elbow was at ear level. He was pushing so hard on his Crayola.

Unbeknownst to Dick, Miss Hammer was starting her strut down the aisle to check our work and solidify her authority posture. She glanced at Dick's "work" and screamed, "Dick Sunman, WHAT ARE YOU DOING!!!!????"

Dick replied, "I'm making a big red airplane just like Jerry said you wanted."

Miss Hammer, her eyes on fire, turned to start on me. Before she could say anything, I took the offensive. "Miss Hammer, Dick never listens to your directions. He always asks me what to do. I'm sick and tired of having to always tell him what to do."

LONG PAUSE!!!!

Dick was immediately moved out of the alphabetical "S" and "U" section of the room and moved to the front of the room. I expect Miss Hammer got loads of laughs telling the story in the teachers' lounge that day!

Through the many challenging years to follow, I have worked on improving my "understanding and patience" skills.

The P.S. to this story - I don't remember Dick ever speaking to me again!

A Memorable Office Tour

The intercom light flashed on my office phone. My boss said "Jerry, come on in, I've got someone here I'd like you to meet". Ten years had passed since I was hired as his first intern. I had been promoted to the Director of one of the four departments in the office - the Political Department.

During the first of three decades in Birch Bayh's Senate service, he had acquired an outstanding legislative and political record. He was viewed as a "must visit" for young Democrats hoping to become part of the next wave of "hot young Washington personalities." This was one such visit.

Our visitor wanted to pick Senator Bayh's brain on political and governmental subjects, details on moving his family to Washington, and various Committee assignments and personalities in the Senate etc.

He was attractive, quick, smart, and had a smile that went from ear to ear. The Senator and I were very impressed. As the meeting concluded, the Senator asked me to give our visitor a tour of the office, introduce him to our staff, and explain our structure and organization. Later in the afternoon, the Senator buzzed me and said, "I really liked that guy. Why don't you do some research and see what his chances are of winning?"

I wrote a one-page memo that stressed the following points:

"Our friend is a county commissioner from a state with only three counties - not thought by many to be a likely path to the U.S. Senate. He is running against a three-term incumbent who is thought of as Mr. Republican by his state's citizenry and he currently enjoys a 60 percent plus approval rating. The consensus of the political experts is, that while our friend has a future in public service, it will not likely begin in the Senate next January."

The young man we met that day WAS elected to the U.S. Senate 48 years ago. On the 20th of January 2021, he was inaugurated as the 46th President of the United States. His name, of course - Joe Biden.

The Tie That Binds

In February 1963, my wife and I moved from Indiana to Washington, D.C. Through a combination of fortunate circumstances, I was hired by newly elected Indiana Senator Birch Bayh. I was his first intern and spent 10 years on his staff during which I had a front row seat to some of the interesting events of the tumultuous 1960s and 1970s.

One such event was a truly historic one in which I contributed to a personally memorable, although historically irrelevant role. Senator Bayh was a political shooting star with three-decade staying power.

He was elected Speaker of the Indiana House of Representatives at age 30, while still attending law school at Indiana University. He was elected to the United States Senate at the age of 37 and he spent three terms in the Senate. One historian characterized him as, "One of the most consequential lawmakers of the 20th century ... responsible for Constitutional Amendments and a list of legislative accomplishments that changed and improved America."

One of the first accomplishments was the 25th Amendment to the United States Constitution regarding Presidential inability, disability, and succession. The Amendment received considerable attention as an alternative to President Trump's impeachment.

My story focuses on a piece of memorabilia from my collection of political items - a tie which can only be described as moderately ugly. The genesis of the tie dates back to 1967.

As the time neared for the Senate vote on the 25th Amendment, I asked if I could attend the Senator's Senate floor debate preparation meeting. The Senator approved my request.

The morning of the scheduled Senate debate, the Senator's staff arrived at the office unusually early and began peppering the Senator with every tough question with which the Senator might possibly be confronted. As time went by and the questions began to trail off, one of the more senior staff members said, "Senator, I think you're ready. But the tie you have on is really ugly. Jerry is wearing a beautiful red, white, and blue tie that would be perfect for this occasion."

Senator Bayh and I agreed, and we exchanged ties. He headed to the Senate floor to lead the debate that had been successful only 24 times in American history - amending the United States Constitution. The Amendment passed and in due time was ratified by the States. The Senator and I never again discussed the exchange of ties.

I've saved his tie all these years. Why did I save the Senator's tie? Maybe the next time my grandchildren visit, I'll show them "the tie that binds the Udell family to the United States Constitution."

Making New Friends

I really enjoy talking to complete strangers. My reputation is known by everyone in the family. Once on a family vacation at the beach in Rehoboth, Delaware, we were trying to divide up into clumps of kids and adults to head out. None of the proposed destinations appealed to me, so my older granddaughter, who happened to be five at the time, said, "Pop, why don't you just sit on a bench on the boardwalk and make new friends." I certainly did. And both the family and I had a good time.

Not all my adventures are memorable, but some are.

Airplanes, as uncomfortable and as inhospitable as they are today, are among my favorite hunting grounds. I do have a rule that I strictly follow. I attempt to start each "new friend" conversation by asking the "candidate" three questions. If my seatmate doesn't pick up on them, I assume he/she wants to sleep, read, or just "veg" out. No problem, it's just three strikes and you're out with my part of the game.

Once I was seated next to a young Latina serving in the U.S. Army. Although she spoke less than perfect English, she seemed receptive for a conversation. I asked her what her job was. (I assumed it would be clerical or medical related.)

She replied, "Demolition."

I questioned, "I think I know what that is, but could you be more specific?"

She answered very matter-of-factly, "We spend most of our time at the firing range. When a round doesn't explode, we go out and disarm it. You can't have a bunch of duds laying around on the range."

Somehow, "Thanks for your service." didn't seem quite enough.

Before we landed, I found some verbiage to convey how impressed and grateful I was. She disarmed explosives for a living in her service to our country! Wow!

My favorite "new friend" story was also in an airplane. An older gentleman was seated in the aisle seat directly across from me. He was wearing a 10-gallon hat. We were seated in the smoking section. When he lit his cigarette with his lighter in his right hand, I could not help noticing he was wearing a Super Bowl Ring! (For those who have never seen one they are massive - they are about three inches square of diamonds!)

As a big football fan, my mind was racing. Who is this guy? This may be my chance to get my insider questions about America's most popular sport answered. The chance of a lifetime! He is too old to be a recently retired player. He's more likely to be an owner or a coach.

No sensible words came to me. Finally, in desperation, I blurted out, "I couldn't help but notice you are wearing a Super Bowl ring. With what team are you associated?"

He smiled, extended his right hand toward me while removing the ring with his left and handed it to me and said, "Ah, my son gave this to me after he won his fourth."

"My son is Terry Bradshaw." (A four-time Super Bowl winner with the Pittsburgh Steelers, NFL Hall of Famer, and an NFL commentator on television.)

Not all my "new friends" are this interesting, although I do learn something from all of them. And once in a while, I hit the jackpot!

One Lesson Two Examples

After thirteen years on Capitol Hill on the staffs of Senators Birch Bayh (D-IN) and Mike Gravel (D-AK), I joined the American Retail Federation, a lobbying and public relations organization devoted to pursuing retail interests in Washington.

As Vice President for State and National Associations, one of my tasks included presenting the "What's really going on in Washington" speech to state meetings of the groups. As a wonderful fringe benefit of my job, I visited all 50 states.

On one trip, I just finished my presentation to the Florida Retail Federation and was looking forward to a relaxing meal alone in one of Miami's gigantic historical resort hotels. The dining room could seat at least a couple hundred guests.

During my meal, I noticed on the other side of the room a young Latina, cheerfully and as rapidly as possible moving from table to table. Her job was to serve the house salad to about one-third of the room.

She did her job with such an efficient grace and dignity, moving fast, but without running and with a pleasant smile. In other words, she made her job look easy and conveyed pride in her work. She left a wonderful impression that brought credit to herself, her manager, the restaurant, and the hotel.

As I left the dining room, I introduced myself to her and told her that I had never seen anyone as outstanding at her job. Although she had not served my table, I shook her hand and passed her a $5.00 tip. By now I realized she spoke little English. But her use of "Gracias" and the tears that welled up in her eyes told me she understood my appreciation of her work.

Many years later, in a totally different setting, my family and I had a similar experience that stressed the same life lesson.

One of my grandsons was born in a Virginia hospital with a very unusual physical condition - not life threatening, but serious enough to require several years of hospital visits, check-ups, and treatment. The initial operation was unsuccessful as was the second.

The third operation was performed at Johns Hopkins by perhaps the world's greatest expert in the field. The operation was successful, and my grandson remained in the doctor's supervisory care until his retirement.

We made many visits to Hopkins through the years. One sparked a reminder of the "world's greatest salad server" lesson I had learned so many years ago in Miami.

As we turned the last block while walking to the hospital, we came upon an older gentleman sweeping up cigarette butts and small trash. He looked up at us, smiled, and stated, "Did you hear? WE are still Number One!" We did not understand what he was saying, but we smiled and continued on. We were in a hurry to visit my grandson.

When we entered the hospital lobby, we immediately understood. The walls of the lobby were covered with signs proclaiming, "Hopkins voted Number ONE again!" We were unaware that for several years,

"U. S. News and World Report" yearly ranks America's hospitals, and Hopkins had been named Number One again!

The fact the maintenance man felt part of the team which included some of the greatest medical minds in the world - and was proud to declare to a hospital visitor that, "WE are still Number One!" says volumes about the culture of excellence possessed by the leadership of the Hospital - and of the Miami hotel I visited so many years ago.

It reminded me of a quote I read in a book on leadership.

The author declared, "There are no trivial jobs in any successful organization. Every one of our employees is an essential employee. If you treat them that way...they will accomplish whatever you have put in front of them."

The CEOs of the Miami Hotel and Johns Hopkins, the salad server at the Miami Hotel and the custodian at Johns Hopkins - they all got it! Excellence can be pursued at every level of any organization. There are no non-essential employees.

The author of the quote: Colin Powell - National Security Advisor to the President, Chairman of the Joint Chiefs of Staff, Four Star General, U.S. Army

Last Day First Day

My last professional employment was as the Director of Development for the Citizens for Sound Economy - a responsible conservative, pro-business group that lobbied for tax and budget legislation at the state level and worked to install pro-business judges at the state and local levels. My job was to serve as liaison to members who administered their company's six figure yearly contribution to the organization.

My first day on the job started with desk-to-desk introductions by my boss to my new colleagues. During this process, I became aware of a going-away party being held for a very popular senior executive after work in the conference room. My boss suggested it would be a good opportunity for me if I chose to attend.

Introductions over, I went to my office. In midafternoon, a young staffer appeared at my office door brandishing a congratulatory card for the day's honoree and asked for a nice note and my signature. Despite the fact that I didn't know the man, I took the card, opened it and turned it over, looking for the least obvious blank space to sign. Much to my horror, there was only one vacant spot on the card. It was directly in the center of the card. When the honoree opened his card, my message would be exactly where his eyes would take him.

I filled the spot with as tasteful but innocuous message as I could concoct. Despite my best efforts, I could think of no one but John Hancock who inscribed his oversized autograph on the Declaration of Independence so large the king could read his name without putting on his spectacles which of course gave birth to one of America's most familiar phrases used when being asked to sign any legal document, just sign your "John Hancock" right here!

My mind was out of control and out slipped the thought, "Maybe no one will notice - yeah, right!" It would more likely be, "Can you believe the new guy? He signed the card right in the middle - some nerve!"

As the party wound down and several staff were offering fond personal and professional reminiscences, one said, "John, ten years from now, when you look back on your time here, what thoughts are likely to come to your mind?"

Without missing a beat, John picked up and opened the card, and answered, "I'm sure my first thought will be - Who in the hell is Jerry Udell?"

I regret I didn't get to know John. I would have liked him and his quick wit and sense of humor. I hadn't met him before and I've never met him again!

The Washington Post

The Washington Post is truly one of the world's great "newspapers of record." It lives up to former editor Ben Bradley's definition of what a newspaper should be - "A first draft of history."

At the time when American newspapers are dying at an alarming rate, the daily edition of the Post is regularly over 50 pages with the "who, what, where, why, and how" of the nation's and world's billions of people and their governments comings and goings.

I find one of the Post's most interesting and informative sections to be the obituaries. It illustrates the fact not all the impactful news is made by elected officials or the famous and wealthy. Indeed some of the most impactful moments of our history occur when an unknown person's life intersects with unplanned circumstances with profound results.

Such a person and her actions were recalled in the December 29, 2021, issue by obit writer Emily Langer.

In 1971, a few years after being advised by a law school dean not to enter law school "because it would be too difficult for a woman," the 26-year-old woman's legal resume included, "uncontested divorces, wills for people with no money, and an adoption for her uncle." Not a likely record to suggest she was about to bend history itself.

Just a few years after the advice, in front of her sat nine jurists in black robes in a Washington D.C. courtroom. The courtroom was the U.S. Supreme Court. The woman's name was Sarah Weddington. The issue was a woman's constitutional right to an abortion. (For trial purposes, the aggrieved party had changed her name from Norma McCorvey, a 22-year-old unwed mother, to Roe).

Weddington won the case 7 to 2 - and thus began America's half-century entanglement with the abortion issue. She died the previous week in her native Texas at age 76.

The obituary author, Emily Langer, fleshed out several other non historically relevant but interesting facts. Weddington herself had an abortion in Mexico several years before Roe was argued.

She served as a member of the Texas State Legislature for three terms and then became the General Counsel for the U.S. Department of Agriculture appointed by President Carter. In addition, she served as a presidential adviser on women's issues. She taught many years at the University of Texas at Austin and the Texas Women's University.

In a curious reversal of prospective, Norma McCorvey and Sarah Weddington became bitter political enemies as "Roe" became a born again Christian and an outspoken anti-abortion advocate.

The publication of obituaries by "The Washington Post" fills in the American tapestry in the most interesting ways - as Paul Harvey used to say, by telling you, "The rest of the story."

Special Relationships

Twenty-six years ago, my pregnant daughter, Laurie, called to notify us to head to Philadelphia the next day and, if all went as planned, we could meet our first grandchild.

My wife, Mare, and I arrived at the hospital and were escorted to a birthing room. Cuddled in my daughter's arms was Abbey, as rosy as Santa's red suit, sleeping soundly and 100 percent healthy! My wife and I gathered around Laurie and Abbey, hugging and sobbing our eyes out as the full wonderment of the miracle of birth engulfed our family.

It became obvious at an early age that Abbey was an "old soul" as she exhibited an amazing amount of empathy and sensitivity as a toddler.

During one visit when she was four years old, the rest of the family left leaving me as the sole babysitter, entertainer, and security officer. I don't ever remember feeling such a weighty responsibility.

After playing in the sand box and a turn on the swing, I asked her what she wanted to do next. She replied without hesitation, "Let's just go somewhere and talk." We decided we should find a "special place" to hold our "special talks."

Although we had to find new locations when the family moved, our "special talks" continued for many years.

The Jury

I am not a lawyer. My only formal education in law consisted of two courses in Constitutional Law as part of my studies toward a Master's degree in Government in the 1960s. I had some practical knowledge of the law during 13 years I spent on two U.S. Senate staffs followed by 17 years with a lobbying trade association. None of this experience was as instructional as what followed a letter I received in July 2009 summoning me to Jury Duty.

One glance at the defendant upon entering the courtroom with my fellow juror candidates revealed to me the case would not be a routine "Homeowner vs. Repair Company" dispute over a botched repair job! The defendant was powerfully built, focused and unemotional. He was flanked by two large State Troopers placed for potential security needs.

The questioning of potential jurors began. The Judge did not tell us how long it might take to select a jury. After a couple of hours, she abruptly declared, "I see we have reached our number necessary to convene the jury, and since we have a few hours left in the day, I suggest we begin the trial."

I had made the jury! The judge continued with a sentence I'll never forget: "I've selected Juror #11 to be your foreman." I glanced down at my juror credential, and sure enough, the number #11 looked right back at me! I bumbled through a fairly incoherent, but respectful refusal, and she courteously replied, "The Court staff will assist you and you'll do fine." "Mr. Prosecutor, please begin."

The case at hand involved a chance meeting at the Wheaton Plaza Shopping Center. The defendant was the gang leader of the local chapter of the Bloods, a nationwide black gang. The local gang had inadvertently run into members of a rival Latino gang, the MS13. Taunts, and insults were exchanged. Someone suggested, "Let's take this outside."

Several witnesses testified the defendant gave the command, "Bust Them!!" - gang translation for "Shoot Them!"

As the chaos began escalating, a mother drove her daughter, who was on her college Christmas break, into the parking lot looking for a parking place.

The testimony confirmed as many as five shots were fired in ten minutes. Three MS13 members, who were in the process of drawing their weapon of choice - machetes - were hit but none was seriously injured. (One could not help thinking of the old admonition about not bringing a knife to a gunfight!)

One bullet hit the mother's car window. Though neither she nor her daughter was struck, the bullet traveled directly in front of their faces and exited through the opposite car window.

The defendant was charged with 22 different counts. Among them: Use of a Handgun in a Crime of Violence; Reckless Endangerment; Attempted Homicide; Attempted Voluntary Manslaughter, and First and Second Degree Assault.

As a result of our deliberations, the defendant was found guilty on all 22 criminal counts.

Our jury seemed to be as diverse as possible given the selection process. While race, occupation, and age divided us, we were firmly in agreement that our responsibilities were to follow the facts wherever they led us and to apply the letter of the law in accordance with the Judge's instructions.

Everyone, without urging of the Court, took these responsibilities very seriously. No one complained about being forced to serve on jury duty. No one napped during the laborious testimony. We "got" the responsibilities the American jurisprudence placed on us.

While no one asked us (the jurors) to rate our performance, I am sure we would have given ourselves a high mark. Although we did not always agree, we worked out our differences.

I'd like to think if our Founding Fathers were looking down on our group of jurors as we disbanded, they would have been pleased with our performance. Some of them might have even said, "They got it! Job well done!!"

A Traveler's Notes

I have been in all fifty states.

I stood atop the Arch in Saint Louis and seen where jazz was born in New Orleans.

I felt the majesty of the Colorado Rockies and walked the Freedom Trail in Boston - and have seen the Old North Church where it was "One if by land and two if by sea."

I felt the pulse of New York and the opulence of Las Vegas. I have seen what Disney created in Florida and God in the Grand Canyon, Alaska, and Hawaii.

I experienced the inspiration of Monticello, the grandeur of Mount Vernon, and the awesome dignity of Mount Rushmore.

And I stood on the hallowed ground in Bunker Hill, San Antonio, Gettysburg, and Pearl Harbor.

Gettysburg where 23,000 men paid the supreme sacrifice to prove this nation would not live half slave and half free.

The USS Arizona, commemorating December 7, 1941, where 3,500 dead, missing, and wounded set forth the chain of events destined to reshape America, the world, and history itself.

I assure you without reservation, from sea to shining sea, America is beautiful!

But if you want to see America's future - look in the mirror.

As Herman Melville declared, "The greatness of America is not to be found in its doctors, lawyers, or politicians ... but in its common people."

For you see, it is the common people in America who bestowed with the blessings of a hard won freedom - with a spirit to know the unknown, challenge the invincible and accomplish the unattainable. Under these circumstances the common man becomes the uncommon American.

About the Author

Jerry was born in Indianapolis, Indiana on December 30th, 1939, and enjoyed a wonderful childhood - thanks to two great parents. His first instruction on the importance, beauty, and power of the written word took place in Sophomore English class where he was required to write one essay and two précis a week. In college, Jerry's favorite academic activity was researching and writing the term papers required by his history and government professors.

Jerry and his wife, Marilyn, moved to Washington DC where he joined the staff of freshman U.S. Senator, Birch E. Bayh (D-IN) as his first intern which afforded him the opportunity to shake the hands with six U.S. presidents. They currently reside in Leisure World and enjoy frequent visits with family and friends.

CHAPTER 5

WANDERLUST AND WORDS

By Richard Eisner

Some Thoughts and Some Tunes
And A Rhyme or Two
A Story That's Nice
And Some Dribble for Spice
A Literary Tease for You

The Need to Be Right

Should I be ashamed to be an American?

I'll start this essay with a question. Is the NEED to be right uniquely American or even human? I am not a social scientist. Although I am fascinated by groups. From insect instincts to interactions of the higher species including us'n.

There are two stories from the animal kingdom that are stuck in my head. One about ants. One about apes. Ants work together for the common good. Their society's success is based almost entirely on their colony's cooperative instincts. No individual ant has the will or tenacity to lead or conflict with another. These traits seem to be uniquely human. Watching ants ruin a picnic or simply around their hill, fire ants in the jungle, or simply foraging on your porch ... there seems to be some unspoken (a human word) coordination among them. It is captivating and something humans can learn from.

Apes, it seems, have a more distinct authoritarian hierarchy. This seems to be the case in higher intelligent mammals. Certainly wolves display a pack hierarchal mentality, as do many other species. As for the ape story, as the colony grew in population all was copacetic and organized until the population grew to an unmanageable size. Then, fights for domination arose within the sub groups. Does this portend for a conclusion that population growth contributes to a break down in society?

Another story comes to mind of a small tribe in rural Africa. The children were enticed to compete for a prize. The researcher set up a situation whereby the winner of the competition would receive a food bit. When confronted with the competition, much to their surprise, the children held hands at the start signal and moved together as a group toward the purse, thereby insuring a shared distribution. As an American, this is unheard of. In my experience as an American, if one is not #1, one is nothing.

Recently, I was engaged in two consecutive conversations, whose contexts were remarkably similar, however, the contents were diametrically opposed. I respect both of the men for their values and life choices, which are necessarily very different. The one gentleman is college educated, well-read and well-spoken. The other ... not so. Not stupid by any stretch of one's imagination. Street smart, not book learned. Both have raised successful children and have had conventionally successful careers. Each is a credit to their respective communities, which are also necessarily very different. One background is urban the other rural.

What I found uniquely similar in these conversations, both these gentlemen had a very narrow view of the world. Their words were remarkably similar in terms how they would 'fix the problems' facing America, yet somehow their myopic vision kept them isolated to the environment in which they are familiar. Thereby limiting the 'FIX' to what works best for them. I observe it all the time in traffic or at the supermarket. The self-centeredness is obvious all around us every day. Common examples ... not signaling one's turn makes me nuts. Parking on the lines instead of between them ... ARGH! Leaving ones cart in the middle of the crowded aisle to look for something three cart lengths down in the freezer section is incredibly inconsiderate.

What occurred to me as I lay in bed waiting to be overcome by sleep was the similarity in the adamancy regarding ENTITLEMENT. Their assumption, or rather need for being RIGHT. Moreover their lack of caring regarding how their beliefs (read actions) affect others. Their lack of regard for other points of view and other life styles. It seems to me that with all the rhetoric, no one is talking about CONSIDERATION or COOPERATION or TOLERANCE or ... you get it yet? Getting along is about principles. ACCEPTANCE of divergent attitudes. EMPATHY seems to be non-existent anymore.

I have always been a pacifist. I have always leaned liberal. No news there to anyone who knows me. In this divisive moment in the history of our Republic, I believe it is incumbent on every member of our society to be more broad minded in their beliefs. If one is an ardent believer in the 2nd amendment, so be it, fine, yet modern technology and machining techniques makes the literal translation incredibly dangerous. (I say for those who have a vigilante mindset.) Free speech is grand. Nevertheless, misinformation, false information, wrong information is like yelling FIRE in a crowded movie theatre. And I think this is where the line needs to be drawn. Especially given such easy availability to social media because of its incredible reach. As a divisive modern society we all must be vigilant. The spirit of the constitution must be adhered to and that is for the protection of all individual rights and beliefs.

ADDENDUM:

Herein is my NEED TO BE RIGHT: For individuals ... be considerate. Across the board, be considerate: Signal your turns. Get your shots. Say thank you and please 5% more. Stop at yellow lights 5% more. Count to 10 5% more instead of RE-acting and knee jerking responses to nonsense. You know ... 5% less of crap and irritation, 5% more of tolerance and cooperation. Then when that becomes our norm, do it all again. What a wonderful world we can become!!!!

September Love

Softly she lay asleep
Embraced in silk and satin silence
A cat nestles gently
In my place.

The fan hums to cool the summer heat
This night untold passions merely steep
Longing breaks the stillness of the stars
Across the hills our love fills the space
I see her face

REFRAIN

Dream, somehow I feel her
Whispering softly, breathing my name
In her thoughts I'm with her in seconds
Our lives mostly sane.

With each kiss I blow into the breeze
I know she waits patiently for me
Knowing someday soon we two will be
Entwined as springtime vines upon a tree
Her love is my key

REPEAT REFRAIN

With fear of ever awakening our love grows higher than even the sky
Every instant our dreams merge together
All the world seems to be, our world seems to be
...Just right!

Junior and Sly

In my formative years, when trying to figure out what to do with the rest of my life, a question that still remains in the forefront of my 'semi-functioning-synapse-lapsed' labelled brain, now 50 odd years later, I was employed as a rock and roll engineer. Prior to this esteemed position at the only 'A' list studio in NYC, one of only three in the world with this reputation and attraction, my stepping stones started with my first studio gig which was mostly cleaning toilets and answering phones in a jingle house. *Jingle house* is the term given to a studio that is primarily involved with ad and commercial production. Procedurally, recording sound for an ad is not much different than the steps involved with creating music. The difference is scale. And yet, while in the studio on off hours, and under the tutelage of my dear friend and mentor, chief engineer Jimmy, I took the opportunity to do some of my own recording and mixing. Believe it or not, some of those cassettes are still in my library and, even more unbelievable in decent listening condition! Although listening now, and being a bit more critical, I have to admit ... the engineering quality left a bit to be desired.

Moving up from the jingle house I found employment as a roadie and SRO engineer (Sound Reinforcement Operator) creating sound and touring with the likes of Aretha, Mandrill, Sly and The Family Stone, Mary Travers, Cheech and Chong, and the indefatigable Chaka Kahn, among others. These months were not fun. They were grueling. They were demanding. The pay was relatively rank. And ... it was a thankless but critically important gig. Most of the time I could be found behind the steering wheel of a fully loaded semi ... in the wee hours of the morning, way before dawn ... racing to the next back stage entrance ... empty said semi ... set the stage and all that implies ... attempt to catch a quick sleep in a dingy hotel room while the next bed was being used as one might imagine it to be used in that situation in that era ... fall awake after the set ... repack the semi only to repeat the mind bogglingly irrational process again 4 hours later. Still, in this position I was connected to the top echelon of Rock and Roll royalty. Lucky me!

There was this one gig in Atlantic City, NJ in which Sly and The Family Stone was headlining. By queer coincidence, this was the first and only gig in which I actually was *THE* sound man. Sly had a reputation of being notoriously late and this date was no exception. After dealing with the entire set up process, it turned out that the backstage sound guy, my up-line supervisor got sick, leaving me to handle that responsibility. Fatigue be damned! This was a career opportunity for me. I grabbed a couple of uppers, very available in those days, and approached my new duty as awake as I could be ... under the circumstances.

The theatre was filled to capacity. There were about 20,000 people in attendance this eve. The senior engineer and I seemed to be the token colored, he being an Arian blonde and me an afro sporting kinky red head. After about an hour and 10 minutes, I sensed the crowd was beginning to lose its patience. Only a few short moments later I get a call on the head set ... "Yo, Scot", Junior was using my nickname Scot. "Yo, Scot ... I gotta check something in the box." The box was our term for a storage unit in the truck which had housed back up equipment in case of mechanical failure. Why he didn't send me became obvious only after the gig. I was so naive then! "C'mon out and keep an eye in the board for me while I take care o' dis business, K?" I did as I was asked. The subsequent minutes seemed an eternity as the crowds' anxiety kept building. Another nerve racking fifteen minutes slowly crept by and then ... all of a sudden ... the mass of people loudly and wildly reared to their feet. Nervously, I turned my gaze from the control board toward the stage as Sly and entourage bounded onto the stage. Holy crap, I thought. Then, with a smirky grin, I pulled up the faders, lowered the lights and voila ... *I WAS ON!*

As I think back, I'm proud to say the evening proceeded flawlessly. However as it came to an end, and the throngs of people dispersed, I was relegated back to the unheralded title of "ROADIE" and found my way onto the stage to coil wire, to pack up microphones and amplifiers, etal, stuff it all into the truck and off again I drove to some nondescript stage door somewhere in America. Good times? Hell yeah!

Several decades after that evening had transpired Junior and I met, purely by coincidence, at a lecture in Los Angeles. In spite of the many years lapse, I recognized him across the room as he entered. I then confronted him with my smirky grin, the same expression and attitude as that evening in Atlantic City. Standing eyeball to eyeball, preventing him from leaving my sphere of influence and without reintroducing myself, I disclosed to him "You owe me big time!" He stepped back protecting his personal space and stared into my eyes for a moment. There appeared another moment of brain search and finally recognition. His face softened and he said emphatically, "Yes, I do!" Subsequently, we had a long overdue make up dinner (on him) and after, as too often does, our lives diverged once again.

Goodbye Tonya

I wanted to grow old with you

Then you found something else to do

It touched your soul. It made me blue

I wanted to grow old with you.

The Middle

"It's a beautiful Friday mid-afternoon. Gonna be a good weekend." I thought looking around the shop. All seemed to be in order. Martin (pronounced MARR-TEEN') and Franco (rolled RRRR's) are cleaning their respective benches indicating their to-do lists are complete. It's nearing the end of the work week and I'm usually a little loose on Fridays. Anyway, neither would ever leave without completing their daily due.

Since my mentors' retirement, I had been thinking about continuing in his path. It was a prudent career move. Additionally, he had offered support setting up: Machinery, contacts, consultation availability ... no brainer. After a short search I found an affordable loft on 36th St. and 9th Ave. It is shared with Stephen, a contractor who leases one third of the space since opening a little over a year ago. And thus ... 'NO NAILS' was born. As the moniker implies, I maintained a no nails old world-y concept of craftsman style furniture and design. My fresh crew consisted of the aforementioned Martin and Franco whom I inherited from my despotic German mentor Gunter. They are both highly skilled, giving me a valuable edge above the competitive fray. Franco is his nick name. Nick names are the norm here. I like things loose and friendly. My moniker is Froggy. If someone comes into my office with a "Mr. Schultz" or even an "Arnold", I may become wary of the next words. "Yo, Frog ..." is the usual when my attention is needed.

I said "good night" and "have a good weekend" to all on the floor as I passed each of their benches. Finally, I crossed through the open doors of the waiting elevator. Big sigh. I pressed G. The doors close.

The Subway

Standing on the downtown platform of the IND station under the New Yorker Hotel at 34th St. and 8th Ave. I took a deep breath. Very deep. Inhaled fully through my nose extending my arms up over my head, stretching up and behind, then exhaling all of it through my mouth quickly and forcefully. Actually, it's been a relaxing day. Looking uptown along the tracks for lights, "I must've just missed the train. It seems I've been waiting a while." I say barely audibly to myself. Turning, I slowly walk back along the platform, hands clasped behind me, thinking about the meeting ahead, then, after a few steps, stopping to stretch again.

Something across the tracks caught my eye. In the middle of the uptown platform, despite the crowds being thin this day. "I can't quite make it out." I whispered to myself. "Something seems to be floating in space, wending its way through the people." I'm trying to focus. It's a ... colorful sailor's hat ... on a small person. Like the one I gave Tonya the last night in New Hampshire. Smiling ... with a fond memory. Summer of TALL SHIPS. 1976. Our grand bicentennial. Then again, a little more audibly, to no one in particular "Just a couple of years ago. It was quite a summer. She was quite a woman. Hmmm. Sigh!" People were looking at me. I turned to look back up the track and shook my head. Wow, I haven't thought of her since that summer.

I looked across the platform and focused hard. This little person seemed oddly familiar. We were almost across the tracks from each other. It was a woman. A beautiful woman very much resembling ...

The (Re)Meet

"Holy Crap!" I thought, now staring. She looked across the tracks at me. Our gazes locked. "Holy Crap!" I thought. "She's smiling now." Another moment passed "... Now ... she's waving." I ... I ... ayeyeyeayye ...! I pointed to the stairs to the mezzanine. We met and embraced. Within four hours the population of my tiny studio apartment doubled. Maybe only a few hundred square feet, but with a million dollar NYC bonus ... out my window ... a bedroom sized terrace. Being this was the attic space, when this building was a family home 100 years ago, out my window is the roof of the one bedroom apartment below. Now it was lined with planters full of color and edibles. There were no high-rises for several blocks south engorging me with sun all day long. No ... we did not immediately make love. Instead we gazed into each other's eyes at length, we held hands too. We walked the dog in Riverside Park before sunset. We sat in the hammock on the terrace and nursed a bottle of wine, still locked in each other's eyes. As night fell I dropped the Murphy bed, we laid down wrapped in each other's arms and then, after waiting what seemed an eternity, we were finally one.

Saturday was a lazy day catching up. Food shopping at Zabars and Dagostinos, then gourmet antics in my tiny excuse of a kitchen to sustain through an afternoon of flirtatious banter and adult play. The morning slipped past noon, then evenly into evening. Nestling in each other's arms after a movie we sleep. Sunday morning she wakes early. Slowly stirring, the aroma wafting through the room sends me back. I'm waking to the fine aroma of my favorite breakfast. The months speed by.

... The last 6 months have been effortless and efficient. My work is going very well. The shop is extremely busy. I've taken on two more journeyman. The business is arguably better than simply staying above water. The relationship, oh my word, impeccable, ... everything is ideal. Tonya has started coming to the office twice a week to assist with clerical duties. This is probably the most positive time of my life. I'm 28, looking forward to years of perfection ahead. ...

The End

... It's not lasting. It's only been seven months of being together and Tonya is showing subtle signs of distress. Recently we've been talking a lot, more than in the previous happy months, touching on deeply sensitive issues. There's an emotional wall deep inside her that I cannot penetrate. She's always kept me away from that part of her with the expert linguistic fluidity of a scalpel in the hands of a skillful surgeon. From these discussions though, I've gleaned some of her concerns. Those that are deep within her, that I have not been privy to earlier. Lifelong concerns everyone goes through. Yet in her empathetic head, everything seems macroscopic. I've been reading as much as I can about her interests and values, her motivations and desires. What motivated her from before we met, from childhood and what changes had she gone through recently that put her on this path. Still, almost imperceptible, I'm feeling it. As this demon, ever so slowly materializes, so is my perfect world dissolving. It won't be long now.

... Now, well into the 8th month we're still civil ... but ... well ... we won't make it to the 9th month. Today I'm helping her pack. In a few moments we'll be riding the subway together down to 34th and 8th Avenue, to where we had reconnected lo those seemingly few months ago, to return to what was formerly the New Yorker Hotel and ... now ... has become the new world headquarters for ... The Reverend SUN MYUNG MOON.

Intro to Copper Mountain

Leaving his home of Pennsylvania was arguably the best decision among a plethora of his awkward life decisions. Stopping at Copper Mountain on a fateful mid-November day added to the excitement of the impending change. It seemed the sun shone brighter in the high altitude clear blue sky. Kyle parked and strutted into the chief's office.

"I'm told yer lookin' fer some good folk with sperience?" He said with a soft, sexy, southern country drawl to no one in particular and to anyone within earshot. In the office sat Cham - the 'overall on snow' guest experience director, Duza - Cham's assistant and Syd - school schedule director. They looked up kinda quizzically. Suddenly a collective shit eatin' grin spontaneously came across all four of their faces, as they all collectively starting hooting loudly. After some time to calm down a more proper Q&A began. It was perfunctory. Nothing compares to the bonding power of spontaneous gut wrenching, tear jerking laughter. And thus began five outstanding ski seasons that changed a life. The change started the next day. Not soon enough for Kyle.

Heading to Los Angeles from Pittsburgh was an easy drive. Kyle wasn't really looking forward to it though. The time at WSXY was pretty cool but it was over. He didn't feel it anymore. His time was spent. He did his thing. His rep was crafted and paid for. Time for a change. The winters at Seven Springs will be missed. Teaching the little ones got to his heart, but not enough to keep him in Steel Town. Kyle had accepted a long overdue offer that came over two months ago. "Those A-holes still want me ... HA! ... and at my price." He said to his reflection in the bathroom mirror, "Yeah ... like that guy said about suckers being born every minute. LOL!"

Something very palpable happened though as he came out the west side of the Eisenhower Tunnel on I 70. Nothing prepared him for the majesty ahead of him. Arguably, one of the most awesome vistas on any of the scores of glorious vistas on this country's maze of Interstates. After putting on his flashers, he slowed and pulled over to the right. Exiting the car, he knelt, kissed the ground, rose up and lifted his arms above reaching as far as he could into the enticing azure. Despite having never been here before, Kyle knew he was home. Weird. Exiting at 205 to gas up, he made a phone call. LA ... no way!

Certainly, Kyle knew he was being watched. Syd and Cham were discrete but ... come on ... any new guy, in spite of his charm and long list of references, still ... there is a probationary period. However that manifests. Sometimes the judgement-ing is obvious and cruel. And sometimes it is matter of fact. Always it is demeaning. Copper was different. Cham ran a tight ship that was respectful and respected. Everyone on the crew truly enjoyed and coveted their position. And Kyle fit right in. Very early on he was accepted into the 'in-crowd' that, after a hard day of teaching, went for their daily beer roasts at CHACH's, just outside the locker room exit. As well, his performance on the hill with clients was exemplary.

"Out of nowhere this competent fresh blood came from ...hmmm ... parts east." Cham was saying to BJ, the resort owner. "Just walked into the office a few weeks ago, with a shopping list of references and clinic stats. We had a few yuks, he left. I'm short handed coming into the holidays donchaknow, so I made a couple o' calls that sounded really good. Seemed like a good bet and ... I think it's worked out in my favor."

"If you like him that much," BJ began saying, while stopping for dramatic moments "I ... uh ... have some good business friends coming up for the end of the year week. Their kids are gonna need to be coddled. There's a gaggle of 'em.' Know what I mean?" He then reached out his hand for his chatter partner. Cham smiled and shook the hand stubbornly waving at his waist. As BJ turned to leave, he gave a kindly grandfatherly wink and smile to Cham.

"Ya wanna see me suh?" Kyle said lounging over the arms of the interview chair, the only seating in Cham's office.

"Yes, Kyle. You've done some good things here. Next week I'll need four instructors for a special group that comes up every season. I'd like you to be on that team. K?"

Kyle snickered. "Well shuah. Sounds like fun."

"Oh it will be. You get to deal with the six kids. Varying ages, all excellent athletes. They're good kids. You'll have fun."

And it was a fabulous fun week. The highlight came on New Year's Eve. For the first time in his career, Kyle participated in the iconic torch light parade. Traditionally every resort has one. Slowly, as the line of torches snaked down toward the Bee Lift base area, and as the crowd became audible, these special kids now became one voice over the din. As Kyle skied closer he seemed to recognize a sound blur ... a word ... no ... a name ... now - his name ... as a chant ... louder and louder ... multi syllabic ... Ky-el, KY-EL, *KY-EL,* **KY-EL,** ... It must have been so very exciting. But then, he was after all, a celebrity ... at least in Pittsburgh. NAH ... this is good. Spontaneous accolades, like an instant standing ovation ... big sigh ... no drug compares.

Goodbye Ashley

A few years before meeting Ashley I had a rather risqué affair with a lovely Brazilian woman, her name was Priscilla. The affair was more intellectual than physical. Our paths crossed for only a brief time, yet there was a continuing mental intrigue that seemed to sustain. It manifested in our perpetual leapfrogging chapters on a fantasy tryst sourced from our experience together, our very vivid imaginations, and our individual needs. We intertwined on a very spiritual level which was both positive and literary. Long after the actual affair waned, her emails tended to continue the story, as did mine to her, each adding to the previous. Our story went on irregularly for about five years. The body of work, unfortunately now disappeared, was quite formidable.

I first saw Ashley at lunch in my colleague's ski class. Our lunch time that day overlapped, as did the level of our students. Therefore, I had the opportunity to catch a glimpse of Ashley out on the hill every once in a while throughout the afternoon. I found her mesmerizing. Typically, after signing out, since our lockers were sorta next to each other, well, opposite sides of the center bench between two walls of lockers, June and I would regale each other with the day's events. I had never taken a personal interest in a student. Unconditionally never one of my own and, until that day, never a colleague's. But, Ashley was the one. I knew it right away. Naturally, I asked June about Ashley. June simply smiled. She was sitting, I was standing slightly behind and left of her at the moment. She titled her head and slyly looked through the corner of her eyes at me. We both laughed.

It was good to see Ashley back again the following day in June's class. We had colluded earlier, if the conditions allowed, our classes would cross paths again at lunch time. The conditions did and we did. I previously gave a note to June to give to Ashley, kinda like a back row thing in a boring high school class between two students not interested in the subject matter in the front. The note was so not appropriate. Still, in the moment, I thought Ashley was worth getting fired for. If that happened, so be it, I'd be free to approach her as an interested single adult. The note was simple and straight forward. "Please consider meeting after class for an apres ski introduction." I signed it simply "an interested friend", giving June permission to answer honestly any question asked. Ashley accepted, without asking anything except the source. *Oh ... my ... word!* I was embarrassed and felt shy and tried to keep my active imagination silent. HA! Like that was possible! I laughed out loud.

Staying professional for the rest of the afternoon took some effort. Not a lot, I am, after all, a very experienced and skillful instructor. This class was at a level that gave me some latitude. My students were strong entry level intermediates, meaning they could link turns and stop as needed or desired on any of the easy/green slopes. Yesterday, after lunch, we crossed into the stage of starting to explore the expanse beyond where early beginners are confined. The confining area is set up to protect and shield the new students from the traffic on the rest of the hill. For all intents and purposes flat, maybe 5 degrees pitch. Its area encompasses about 5 - 10 acres. Outside of the protected area is several orders magnitude grander. What they are now experiencing they've only seen in magazine pictures or movies. As well they'll be skiing over TERRAIN FEATURES. Terrain features, for this group, are: level changes, banks and some steeper pitches. Even the corduroy from the snow cats is a new feel under feet. Every nuance is new and needs appropriate introduction.

First and foremost however, and what is often the most overwhelming, is the vastness. The confined area is well below tree line, the altitude at which tree growth is stifled. It will be the first time these newbies get to the "TOP OF THE ROCKIES", some 2000' above tree line. Their first vistas across the range at 12,000 feet above sea level can be maybe 100 miles. It is truly breathtaking in the winter on a clear day. The resort is almost 6,000 acres, of which

3,000 is arguably within their reach, depending on their individual level of commitment, which in this group is a solid A+, and the length of their individual stay. Should this blessed group stay together at least one more day, I would be able to transition into coach from the mentor I have been since we met and bonded three days ago. I was truly gifted this week! So, this afternoon, while demo-ing certain patterns that are rote for me, I could let my mind wander a tad anticipating what would hopefully transpire after class.

"Everything bodes well", I muttered under my breath on my way to the locker room. "Everybody will be together tomorrow and Friday, then four of the five will stay through the weekend. Not just a nice paycheck, a good time with good people." I got to the locker room smiling. "Let this feeling ride. Let it ride. On a roll. BOOYAH!" I exclaimed. My colleagues looked and giggled like a bunch of seniors the night before prom night in 1957! "Huh, What-up?" I pondered. "Everyone had been through it. Having a great week with a great continuing group." Then, I reddened ... as all my brethren had a roast on my behalf. June wouldn't have breached my trust. "Did I say something to someone?" I thought. We are, in fact, living within a storybook and glory industry culture not much different from the RED CARPET! My colleagues were thinking about tonight. I was thinking about the rest of my life, however. I mean ... I knew it. The moment I saw her, I knew it!

Arrived at Chauncey's about 1615 (4:15 PM for the lay folk). Ashley was at an empty booth with two tequilas at the ready. It was hard to contain my ardor. We weren't there long, just long enough to down the elixirs. Then to the lounge where there was quiet and ambiance. I wanted to talk. I needed to know who this woman was *(my muse come to haunt me?)*, where she came from *(beyond the deepest inclination within my heart?)*, what was the source of her magnetism *(the spell of the ancients?), why did our paths cross now? How did I fall prey to her potion?* All of a sudden it seemed we were alone after talking incessantly for nearly five hours. For me, it was a school night and I take my work very seriously, so, as we slowly walked across the plaza, I took her hand in mine. She did not resist. It was a respectful moment. It was an enchanting and warm moment. "Good night dear

Ashley," I said. She answered in kind. She had reserved one of the quaint rooms in the turret overlooking the BUSY BEE lift for 12 days. This was her eighth night. The remaining nights we were together as romantically but as platonically possible. Needless to say my class that week ended in complete coordination with the emotional high of meeting my mate. Thus began 1 1/2 years of sheer bliss.

For the next 18 months, through times of hardship and times of love; times of tests and times of strength; times of thoughtlessness and times of song; and times of bitterness and times of healing, our love grew exponentially with every breath. I had found the ... ne ... we had found, in each other, our compliment. In mid-life, as if Monsieur Kismet had been guiding us through a dramatic enactment of Hosea 11:4:

> "I led them with bands of human kindness, with cords of love.
> I treated them like those who lift infants to their cheeks;
> I bent down to them and fed them."

A trip to Los Angeles was booked so the two most important women in my life could meet, my Mom and Ashley. We stayed in the guest house of dear friends in Hollywood, the first of the three nights there. Then to a hotel near Mom at the nursing home. She had been there for over three years. It was decided that she give up the apartment in Beverly Hills, for the comfort and security of the home. She had her own room and was still fully independent, although at almost 90 years, her age was taking its toll on her stamina. Ashley and she got along famously. I was elated.

We had a lovely dinner at the hotel and talked about the future. There was no question as to the page we were on. It was the same. I wanted to ask her to marry me right then and there, but ... there is always a but! ... it just wasn't the right time. Something put me off. I needed to ask her on our turf. I needed to ask her on a chair lift or on a horse or on a hike ... in the Rockies. If nothing else, we have bonded in the lifestyle of the top of the Rockies. The night faded into flagrant ecstasy.

In the morning, while Ashley was showering, I was working on the next book chapter for Priscilla. Remember Priscilla? Yes, the novel continues. When Ashley had finished, I exited the window being worked on and went into the bathroom for my shower. On the screen were the titles of the various emails currently in my inbox and the first few words of each in a list. One of them said blatantly "regarding our affair ..." It was the last chapter from Priscilla. Ashley did not know about Priscilla. This was not good.

Ashley is Latina. Latinas are very passionate. Unfortunately, this Latina was also very staid in her ways. She had an abusive history with the men of her past. Suffice it to say, there was nothing I could do or say. She erroneously added me to the list and lost all trust in me. Voila. Bad toggle switch! By the time we had gotten home to Bozeman it was over. I shan't get melodramatic here ... and yet ...

It seemed so right how we met on the hill

I fell so deep as if it were G-d's will

You saw something private and missed its meaning

And then all died, ... I'm dying still.

Bob Awoke

Bob awoke with a start. He looked around the darkened room wondering where he was. A small low wattage bulb shown from an uncovered floor lamp off his right shoulder. In the dim light, he noticed across the room the fraying curtains covering two murky windows ahead of the cot on which he lay. His head ached. His skin was goose pimply. Not unlike a recent reaction he'd had after eating some bad fish. His stomach felt upside down. He was sweating. What happened? He felt as if he were coming down from an awful binge. "Very strange" he mused. "I don't drink or use any intoxicants!"

The ride up to his lakeside home was quite enjoyable, as always. The westerly drive up the long tree lined curved driveway just after dusk was calming and serene. And, if the time of day permitted, he would pull over to admire G-D's artistic grandeur at the designated perfect vantage spot overlooking the lake before arriving at the end of the drive, which he had done this late winters day.

Twice a year, for several weeks, depending in his work schedule, he was gifted with this serene moment. The dimming sky was still alive with color. Lovely reds and oranges bleeding into purples and finally bleeding into a magnificent midnight blue. All this augmented by the sparse cloud cover above the horizon. After parking along the outside wrap around deck in his usual place, he checked his Rolex. "Just a few minutes early. She'll be pleased." he mused to himself. Excitedly, he bounded up the stairs to the front door. He reached for the door knob, opened the large heavy carved oak door ... then nothing ... nothing until this moment of cloudy awakening.

He stroked his finely manicured medium length white beard. Straining his baby blues, looking into the dimness, trying desperately for something to recognize. Checking the time again ... his watch was gone. "What the ..." he thought. He sat up on the edge of the cot. Then the chill hit. The floor below his socks was as cold as the frozen lake. His shoes were gone. "What the ..." again raced through his mind. He put his hands into his pockets. Right pants pocket, in which he kept his cards and currency. He never kept change. Change always found its way into the divided cigar box hidden in the kitchen pantry. Three times a year, since childhood, he'd roll up what was accumulated to deposit into his savings account. Surprisingly, now after almost 50 years, he accumulated close to 10 grand that otherwise would've been foolishly spent on lottery tickets or beer.

His money and credit cards were secure, as were his keys and the mini multi tool found in his left pocket. His phone however, was not in his right rear pocket, where it should be. As far as he could tell in the dim light there was not any form of communication inside the structure. No phone nor computer. Not any modern equipment with which he could contact authorities or, at least his wife. He stood. He listed. He grabbed the edge of the cot as he almost fell over. Straining to stand erect he stretched his arms over his head, reaching for the ceiling, which seemed miles above. He managed a slow 360 trying to find any element around him that would, thrust his memory awake.

Then, slowly, he shuffled toward the door as his eyes became fully accustomed to the dim light. He reached for the door knob, then slowly opened the door. He peered into the eerie blackness of the night. Nothing. "What the ..." again was the comment swarming in his confused mind. Nothing ... as in a scene from Beetlejuice. No deck. No car. No forest. Just space.

He backed up into the structure incredulous. His knees buckled, he turned and fell, landing face down on the cold hardwood floor. He brought his hands to his face in a deep quagmire of confusion ... he wept. Time seemed to have stopped.

"Am I dead?" He said out loud to no one there.

"Is this heaven? Or ... Holy crap ... or ... no, I am ... or rather I was a good person. My work was always conspiring for the benefit of others. Yes."

His diatribe of self adulation continued, "conspired" is the right word. So often his office would find or create a support system for those unfortunates outside of the mainstream."

He then pinched his left forearm hard. "Ow!" He exclaimed. "I felt that!" He exclaimed almost gleefully. "I am an intelligent man. I have a successful business. People look up to me." Then adding louder ... "And, I am hungry!"

Spirits do not do hunger or pain, he thought. His belief system regarding the soul or the universal of consciousness or of collective intelligence in the hereafter could not accept that one's nervous system would not respond if he were ... He let the thought dissipate into oblivion. Therefore, he must still be a breathing functioning Homo Sapiens. Not an amorphous spirit seeking entry into the next realm.

He meandered to the murky windows and peered out into the nothingness. The eerie blackness was beckoning to him. Darkness reaching its powerful arms around him, enveloping him, drawing him near. He consciously ignored the pull. He experienced a physical restraint of a magnitude almost beyond his damaged capabilities. His face contorted as his muscular frame rejected the onslaught of this formless formidable force.

One window was slightly open inviting a small draft. In his minds ear he searched for some symptom of reality. The chirp of crickets or the croaking of frogs. The din of aircraft or distant foghorns across the lake. Nothing. How weird.

He took a deep breath, returned to the cot, sat down to collect his thoughts. Slowly he recounted the events that transpired in the last while, despite that he had no reference to time. Where was he? How did he get here? And more importantly, how could he return to whatever constitutes reality?

His favorite literature was science fiction. So ... could he use any of those fictional themes as an armament or maybe ... a conveyance? Fictional was the operative word. Did he find a hole in the time/space continuum? Did he fall through some sort of time/space tunnel into a parallel world? "Nnnoooo!" he screamed. "I am not ready for this weirdness. There is simply too much still to do in my world." He lay prone and stared up into the darkness. Sleep came uneasily.

In the silence of the moment Duke Ellington's "Take the 'A' Train" slowly, barely perceptible, began to appear in his mind. Becoming more aware, Bob opened his eyes. There he lay, in his California King cradled in Trisha's arms, staring into her weepy eyes. His wife Trisha couldn't get to him fast enough as he tripped and fell entering their home, crashing his head into their hard wood futon which she had temporarily moved toward the entry enabling her to vacuum that area of rug. Now ... fully awake, Bob smiled.

An Ode to Retirement
WATCHIN' THE TOMATOES GROW

(slow jazzy/bluesy)

Been a long time comin' and it feels so good
We're sitin' at this picnic table made of wood
Next to the hot house watchin' the tomatoes grow
Time don't mean nuttin' to me no mo'.

It's all so simple like the Pennsylvania Dutch
The rat race is behind me, thank you very much

Hasn't been too long since the old daily grind,
Sortin' and deliverin' almost made me blind
Crack o' dawn would find me dressed and ready to be assigned
Crack o' eve would find me draggin', wantin' to resign
But, I'd get up and do it agin if'n I had ta
Proudly spent 35 years bein' a postal worka

REFRAIN

When it was finally time for my pension
... We bought us a farm
City folk stuck in suspension
A log cabin, an out buildin' and a barn
With it came some chickens, two cows and a mule
A vegetable garden and a whole lotta tools

My days are never regulated
I wake and I forage and I eat and play
I'd do my share then sit and rest til I'm sated
Then repeat for the rest of the day
Chores are easier than anticipated
We rented a kid from across the way

Calm as a glass sea, no winds gonna blow
A few wispy white clouds up above don-cha-know
Couple o' lazy dogs sleepin' at my feet
No traffic to contend with, just dirt ain't no street
Now I'm sittin' here with my cup o' joe
Just watchin' the tomatoes grow

REFRAIN 2

Now, a couple of years later
... We're don' just fine
I've learned to be a tractor operator
The wife is busy drinkin' our wine
I'm relaxed and she's still so pretty
Life's so darned good bein' out of the city.

Been a long time comin' and it feels so good
We're sittin' at this picnic table made of wood
Sittin' here with my cup of JOE
Time don't mean nuttin' to me no mo'
Sittin' here with my cup of JOE
Just watchin' the tomatoes grow.

♦ ♦ ♦ ♦ ♦

About the Author

People constantly tell me I've done so much and that I have lived an enviable life. I suppose that's partly true. Next to RENAISSANCE MAN in the dictionary is my picture. To sustain wanderlust, many talents must be developed and honed. I have been a musician and actor; a designer and craftsman; a sports enthusiast, coach, mentor; and now an author. What you have enjoyed are mostly based on moments of real experience. I did, in fact, do that Sly show in Atlantic City being the token color in an aura of, shall we politely say, heavy energy. I don't know who Bob is or where he came from, although I do know Lyle very well! Tonya and Ashley may be the imaginings of a lonely college Sophomore ... or maybe not. My songs ... are for your interpretation. Enjoy.

CHAPTER 6

A COMING OF AGE IN AFRICA

By Don Siegel

Introduction

The following short vignettes constitute pieces of the memoir I am preparing for my children and grandchildren. I've had opportunities to travel far and wide through my profession as a Geologist, and what I experienced during these travels substantially made me what I am today.

Of all of my trips, the one when I traveled at only 21 years old to Kenya proved the most formative. Far away from my orthodox Jewish culture in New York, I gained the lessons in life that remain with me today and continue to profoundly affect how I view the world and personal relationships. I hope you enjoy this little collection of true stories.

A Novel Invitation

My parents never spoke to their friends about my choice to be a geologist, a career path that embarrassed them. The other kids in our community chose degrees leading to medicine, law and business, and other standard professions to ensure a financial good life thereafter.

Near the end of my senior year studying geology at the University of Rhode Island, Paul Abel called me to his office. Two years prior, he had enrolled in the same sophomore level geology class as myself. The other students in the class didn't want anything to do with the 'old' bearded, bell-bottomed hippie who sat at the back of the room. After a short chat, I learned Paul served the university as a professor of organic chemistry, enjoyed paleontology, and simply wanted to learn about fundamentals of sedimentary rocks where fossils occur.

I found the man interesting, if eccentric, and invited him to join with two other friends and me to collectively work on our assigned semester-long research project. In short order, we had full access to Paul's extensive laboratory, including a working still hidden within a maze of blown glass tubes linked to gas chromatographs. At the end of our class, we all earned A's.

Paul lived in a geodesic dome deep in the woods. One weekend, he invited my girlfriend and me to dinner. There, he worked adult magic and in short order had seduced her away from me to indulge in things I would not dare try at the time. Charismatic male professors in the 1960s commonly wooed attractive female students, and naïfs like me simply could not compete. I became angry with him.

Paul noticed me in the Geology Building a few months later and he said while passing, "When you graduate, Don, perhaps you might be interested in going to Africa with me."

"Yah right," I thought.

Two years later during my second senior semester I received a call from Paul, asking me to see him.

"Does he want to apologize for taking my girlfriend?" I thought. *"After all this time?"*

I walked into his office, and he got to the point; "Remember when I mentioned Africa to you two years ago? I'm inviting you to Kenya this summer. You'll be an assistant geologist working with chief geologist Kay Behrensmeyer on the new Leakey expedition. You will need to get there by your own means, but after that all your expenses will be paid by the National Geographic Society." I discovered that Paul worked summers with the Leakey family as their man 'Friday,' recruiting staff and managing logistics.

I was speechless. My family subscribed to the National Geographic Magazine, and we fully knew about the Leakey family's discoveries in Olduvai Gorge that changed anthropology forever. I called my dad and got another surprise; he agreed to send me. My participating on a National Geographic trip with Louis Leakey trumped any traditional career path the other kids might have taken. Dad finally got bragging rights.

Zurich

Recurrent malaria sickened Paul in Zurich during our first stop on the way to northern Kenya. While he nursed himself, I walked from our little hotel past Swiss homes adorned with wood balconies and carved ornaments to the heart of the city. I wanted to buy dinner at the train station's restaurant.

It began to rain, and I sheltered under a big tree's canopy to try and stay dry. Then, a Volkswagen pulled over and a middle-aged woman opened the passenger's side window.

"Wie gehens zie?" she asked.

"Um, zu der Bahnhoft, the train station."

"Steig ins Auto, Ich werde dich dorthin bringen."

She opened the passenger door from within and motioned me to get in. I did not quite understand the German despite studying it in college, however the woman looked friendly enough so I accepted her invitation to help.

"Café?" she asked and pointed to a bakery we approached after a few minutes driving.

"Ja, danke," I said.

"Wie heißt du?"

"Um..Donald."

"Meine name ist Claire," she said, and parked the car.

We ran through the rain into the cafe and sat at a table. She told the waiter something I didn't understand, and he brought towels to help me dry out.

"Woher kommst du."

"Oh boy, this conversation is going to be difficult," I said to myself.

"Vereinigte Staaten."

"Was denkst du über den Krieg in Vietnam? "

"Vietnam, she must be asking me about Vietnam."

I answered in fractured German that I didn't want to go there and fight.

"Hat ihnen Präsident Kennedy gefallen?"

"Kennedy. Kennedy. She's asking me something about President Kennedy."

I said I liked Kennedy.

"So did I," Claire replied in English, "He was an outstanding president to we Swiss."

"You speak English?"

"Yes, Donald, but I appreciate you trying to communicate with me in my own language. Not many Americans do. They assume we speak theirs."

After a pleasant hour talking, Claire dropped me off at the train station for my dinner. The only items I recognized from my German vocabulary were beer, light and dark, and trout - of all things. The trout cost far more than the other items but still seemed cheap given the dollar exchange rate. So, I ordered it.

The waiter then snapped his fingers. Two more waiters ran over to fuss, changed my table linen, and bought out expensive silverware. Everyone in the room stared. Nobody but rich tourists ate trout in the French style and my waiters were delighted. I overheard someone at another table say "Americanish" to laughter.

I looked at the waiter and shrugged but felt somewhat humiliated after feeling so pleased with myself when I tried to speak German. I learned from this experience it's hard to know proper behavior in foreign countries if you don't spend time learning about it before you visit. My gaffs would sadly reoccur again in other foreign countries. I sometimes can be a slow learner.

Benghazi

If you want to fly cheaply to Africa, you do it on charter flights. East African Safari Airlines provided such a service for Paul and me from Zurich to Nairobi. Its vintage prop-liners carried about fifty people. Overweight German tourists shoved through to get on the plane first. I remember their trailing kids shouting, "Vater. Mutter. Wait."

The Germans hogged the front rows; and nervous looking Arabs wearing keffiyehs occupied the seats behind them. Tourists, college kids, and we sat towards the back. I fell asleep and woke up when the plane jolted to a landing, the air conditioning no longer working.

"Benghazi to refuel," Paul said.

I glanced out the window and saw stony desert pavement to the horizon with the sun quivering through heat waves over dunes at the horizon.

"Benghazi at dawn," I said. *"I can't believe I'm here."*

Two men wearing military uniforms walked onto the plane.

"Passports please. All leaving the plane, passports please."

Refueling would take time and we wanted to stretch our legs and maybe get a bite to eat in the terminal.

The soldiers walked down the aisle and I heard them ask, "Jewish? Jewish?"

Outside the window, uniformed men with Kalashnikov rifles were surrounding the plane. I just about lost my bowels. The Israelis had defeated multiple Arab armies, including Libya's just two years prior and I knew what would likely happen if the soldiers found out they caught a Jew.

"Don," Paul whispered, "Say you are German."

A soldier arrived and looked at my passport. "Jewish?"

"No. Ich bin Deutscher."

"Siegel?" He said. "Ein Deutscher?"

"Yes. Ya. Ich bin Deutscher."

He looked closely at me and then returned my passport.

"Good thing he didn't know your name would have been spelled with the 'i' and the 'e' reversed in German," Paul quipped.

We walked into the terminal bar complete with a rotating fan and patrons looking like extras in the movie "Casablanca." Paul ordered a beer and I ordered a soda. We stepped outside to watch the sun move higher with the temperature, stifling by the time we left.

The very next day, Muammar Muhammad Abu Minyar al-Gaddafi violently took over the Libyan government. Landing in Benghazi was my first brush with danger in my trip to Africa. It once again taught me the value of learning a foreign language, even if crudely. A lesson I had not learned well enough in college.

The Great Man

Very few people project charisma so strong that you would do almost anything for them. Dr. Louis Leakey, the anthropologist, was one such person who carried such transcendence and authority.

After our plane landed in Nairobi, Dr. Leakey invited Paul, Kay, and me to dinner and to spend the night at his compound.

Before our dinner, Paul said, "Whatever happens, don't ask Louis about David Pilbeam." The aggressive Yale anthropologist competed with Leakey for prestige in the study of human evolution and had just published a paper about the fossil pre-human, *Ramapithecus,* based on data from a single fossil mandible he said he discovered hidden in the basement of the British Museum. The news media picked up the story and emphasized Pilbeam's acute criticism of Leakey's theories on human ancestral lineage.

We arrived for the meal. Louis invited us into his living room, poured us wine, and excused himself to put the final touches on the beef stroganoff he had personally cooked. Over the meal I answered questions about my geological background and interests, and then complemented the great man on his cuisine, and then just couldn't help myself.

"Dr. Leakey, what do you think about David Pilbeam's discovery? The one I read about in *Time Magazine*."

Paul glared at me, but Louis smiled and sighed.

"David Pilbeam did not *discover* a *Ramapithicus* jaw hidden in the British Museum. He already had published on the same fossil and categorized it unequivocally as an ape."

"Really?"

"Yes, in a rather obscure journal."

"How could Pilbeam do that? Isn't that a lie?"

"Don, people can argue all they want about interpretation of the fossil record, but my careful data and measurements of fossils will stand the test of time," Leakey replied.

We drank brandy after dinner and readied for bed, Kay and I in the circular thatched guest huts and Paul in the main building. I awakened shortly after midnight to a scream, loud, horrifying, and penetrating. And, again and again, as if a live intelligent being were being vivisected by Dr. Moreau. My adrenaline spiked as I lay in bed, eyes wide as the shrieks continued until dawn.

At breakfast after several cups of coffee, I asked, "Dr. Leakey, last night I heard screams. Terrible screams. I was too afraid to leave my room to see what it was."

"Oh, that," he explained, "Just the rock hyrax living in the thatch above you. Mating. Noisy buggers, aren't they? Rodents. Nothing to be afraid of."

"It would have been nice if you told us about them before we went to bed," I thought.

The great man grinned impishly at me: he had played an African practical joke.

Cats shriek too when they mate. I wondered what lions sounded like when they coupled. The thought of hearing them in the bush gave me shivers and it still does. And that is no lie.

A Missed Opportunity

The New Stanley Hotel stands near the center of Nairobi, palm trees growing through its foyer roof in grand style. Paul and I lodged in the comparatively modest Ainsley Hotel, where he was still fighting the symptoms of his malaria and sent me out to find quinine pills.

The bustle, sights, and smells of Nairobi intoxicated me. In the crowded outdoor market, I bartered to buy tiny red bananas, a couple of elephant hair bracelets for luck, and the quinine pills. I saw the New Stanley and walked in, tropical foliage and polished hardwood everywhere. Some men at tables wore pith helmets. "*So that's real,*" I thought. "*Not just in the movies.*"

I walked to the bar and purchased a soft drink. An attractive older woman, at least to my twenty-one-year-old eyes, sat alone at the bar's end and motioned me over. I shyly approached her, wondering what she wanted.

"You're new to Nairobi, aren't you?"

"Yes. I'm here to go on an expedition with Louis, Mary, and Richard Leakey," I blurted.

"The Leakeys: I'm impressed," she said, and smiled. "You must be very smart."

I sat next to her and she elicited more information from me over the next hour; where I grew up, my interests, and so on. In hindsight, the woman offered nothing much about herself. She looked into my eyes and said, "Donald, my husband's away in Europe for the week and I'm alone here at the hotel," and then she put her hand on my knee. "Please come back tomorrow afternoon. Come swim in the pool with me."

I intuitively knew I had zero experience to do what the woman had really offered me, and it wasn't a swim in the afternoon. I became terribly drawn to the opportunity but conflicted at the same time by my Orthodox Judaic upbringing. I suffered a strong contradiction between what I wanted to experience and what my acculturation told me to do.

I did not return to the New Stanley Hotel.

Nonetheless by the end of that African summer, I had embraced multiple contradictions in my decision making, choices that proved sometimes good and sometimes not, but always interesting.

I occasionally still wonder if I should have deliciously discovered the usefulness of accepting contradictions in my life first at the New Stanley Hotel.

Koobi Fora

At dawn we left Nairobi in a Land Rover and first drove on a two-lane highway to the town of Marsabit surrounded by the forested national parkland. We turned a corner in a grove of acacia trees and startled a huge bull elephant. It charged, bellowing, head down. With no place to turn, we prepared for impact. The bull stopped a yard away, shook its head and walked away. The king of his domain, enough said.

A family of giraffes looked on, bemused.

We continued northwest across a vast parched lakebed and saw an African crossing it, only holding a spear. How does he do this without water?

We drove by the tiny crossing of North Horr to an Ileret oasis to refill our water carboys. Along the way, a female cheetah and her two cubs saw us and frolicked in play, leaping, around our vehicle. The glory of these animals.

We stopped near piles of flat rocks to rest a bit from the jarring ride, now over bad gravel. Kay calmly warned, "Look under the slab you're about to sit on, Don." I lifted it, tipping it away from me. A carpet viper slithered out. No antidote.

We arrived at the Koobi Fora camp seventeen hours later after finishing the drive for several hours on dry gravel stream beds instead of roads. The camp's green tents strung out along the shore of the lake.

"I noticed a clothesline hung with strips of meat. What's that?" I asked.

"Zebra. Jerky to eat on the upcoming safaris," Kay said.

"What about the bird shit on it?"

"The sun will kill the bacteria."

And it did.

Silly, my civilized fears about eating.

I bathed in the lake the next morning accompanied by sets of eyes protruding from the water twenty feet away, curious Nile crocodiles. But stuffed with perch and catfish. Almost friends.

A cute momma hippo and her baby lived adjacent to us in a little delta. Africa's most dangerous animal. Recently, another hippo had split a Peace Corp worker in two elsewhere on the lake. I stayed away from the hippos and preferred to swim among the crocs.

Homo Habilis

I had come to Lake Turkana to map the geology where the Leakeys believed that our ancient ancestors, hominids, lived along its shores millions of years ago. But I wasn't so interested in this. Volcanoes and lava were my young scientific passions. Kay would point to a fossil of mastodons, ground sloths, and crocs in the sandstone and shale; and I would point to a lava flow nearby and comment on the beauty of the black rock.

The vertebrae fossil accumulations at Koobi Fora were amazing. We would name them for their dominant species; 'Hippo Valley' or 'Elephant Canyon.' Once a competing paleontologist came to visit and the man's eyes literally bugged out as he picked up a specimen out of many lying in front of him. Richard Leakey, the Leakey's 26-year-old son, took it away and tossed it over his shoulder, shattering behind him on the ground.

"Whhhhaaaat the ...," the scientist began to say.

"We only take the most perfect specimens," Richard replied, in perhaps the best example of scientific upmanship I've ever seen.

Kay discovered a layer of white volcanic ash and saw impressions in it. "My god. These are hominid footprints. And look here: stone tools."

I picked out of the ash a piece of volcanic rock with a serrated edge and shivered. An extinct ancestor of mine literally had made and used this tool. We began to excavate the tool site ash layer.

"But where are the hominids that made these tool and footprints?" Richard asked.

Hominid fossils are the rarest of rare fossils. Richard with several of his African staff set off one day on our camels to explore north of camp while we worked to expose more of the tool site. Several days later we heard a shout.

"They're back."

In the distance the safari advanced at a fast trot, Richard in front wearing his colorful keffiyeh. After he dismounted, he removed two small boxes from his pack and sauntered into the dining tent to greet us. In one box lay a nearly complete skull of *Austropithicus Robustus*, one of the earliest hominids. I held it in my hand and remembered lines from Hamlet:

> *"Alas, poor Yorick! I knew him ... a fellow of infinite jest, of most excellent fancy."*

"And this," Richard said as he pulled out of the second box the skull of *Homo Habilis,* our direct ancestor.

"We now know that *Australopithecus* and *Habilis* lived together, but only *Habilis* survived. They probably made the tools we see."

Indeed.

The unforeseen contingency of Richard Leakey finding two skulls of different hominids living at the same time not only changed the direction of anthropology, but also the direction of my professional life. I was not longer interested in volcanos. Embrace contingencies.

Nguruguru

'Nguruguru.' Say it three times. Does it roll off your tongue, the name of the camel who took me to places where Land Rovers could not go? Richard Leakey assigned me the big bull who lorded over a harem of half a dozen females. I stepped through the thorn fence that corralled him.

"Hello, I'm Don your new rider," I said to my charge.

"Nguruguru," he replied, and projectile-vomited green-yellow bile on me. I retched in turn. Richard named him from the sound of his puking. Funny, right?

On the day of my first camel safari, I pulled Nguruguru's reins and halter hard to the ground, forced him to his knees, and flung myself onto the saddle, two carved posts attached on either end of a padded stool. The animal thrust his back legs straight up and I flew over his head onto the ground, over and over again until I figured out how to stay aboard by leaning far backwards over the rear post.

A running camel moves its front and back left legs forward first, and then its right legs in like kind, swaying the rider side to side. A seasoned sailor could get nauseated, let alone me. On top of it, the motion painfully pounded my testicles and my penis against the front post of the saddle.

"Ride cross legged, balanced like me, Arab-like," Richard shouted from his own camel.

The new position, if feeling unsteady worked until the beast ran me through stands of fish-hooked thorned acacia trees that tore strips of skin from my legs and loosened the straps holding my saddle.

Down to the ground I fell again.

Nguruguru smiled.

I remounted and beat him with a cane when he approached more of the 'wait-a-bit' bushes. He plunged through them anyway.

Enough.

I dismounted and walked the rest of the way to our destination, yanking the beast behind me, the rest of the team far in the distance.

I arrived at our campsite and tied Nguruguru to a stake next to the other camels.

"Put your sleeping bag on the ground outside of the camels to complete our circle," Richard ordered.

"Why outside and in a circle?"

"To protect them. Lions will surely smell them, but they'll get to us first. If they stampede our camels, all of us will die here. Too far to get back home by foot."

That night while everyone slept, I moved my sleeping bag to allow unrestricted passage through our human circle directly to Nguruguru. Discretely, I loosened his rope a bit and tightened those holding the other camels. If the lions arrived late at night, he'd bolt and they'd eat my dumb charge first for sure.

It's nice to find a way to regain personal pride, even if the truth be told, I had already lost the game.

The Loo

At Koobi Fora I slept in my tent on a cot. The mosquito netting at the front and back allowed breezes at night towards the lake to cool me. Our loo was dug a hundred feet uphill. Canvas sheets concealed us doing our private business in the privy.

One night we heard hoofs clatter past and then roars. The local pride of lions had figured out that our tents conveniently formed an artificial barrier to drive topei and zebra. The big black-maned male made the kill at the north end of our encampment as the frightened game ran away from the lionesses chasing them.

After not sleeping all night, I wandered at dawn down the trail to the loo for my morning constitutional. After I arrived at the dining tent for breakfast and others arrived and settled down to eat. Richard Leakey inquired, "Don, did you go to the loo this morning?"

"Mrrmff..yes," I said with a mouth full of scrambled eggs.

"All up. Everyone up. Now." Richard ordered. "We're going for a walk."

He took us down the trail to the loo and pointed to a dismembered topei carcass laying in the beaten-down brush.

Unknowingly, I had startled the lions at their own breakfast, and they miraculously fled.

"Watch where you walk and what you do, damn it," Richard said to us, angry.

I have used that advice ever since, even where lions seem distant. There are other kinds of lions to watch for outside of the African veld.

On Time

Woody Allen said, "Ninety nine percent of life is showing up."

Indeed.

We traveled light when we mapped geology east and north of our camp. Each of us carried a one-pint canteen, an orange, a sandwich, a rock pick, a notebook, and a large empty pack for specimens to bring back to analyze. Before we began work in the early morning, I would drink my fill of 'squash,' a British version of lemonade. Later at high noon, a large goatskin of it would reappear with our Land Rover at a designated pickup spot on the outback road. By then the landscape became too hot to work, well above a hundred-and-twenty degrees Fahrenheit. If we didn't reach the pickup on time, we would be left behind to get back to camp on our own.

One day, Kay and I spent the morning mapping a series of red and grey rock layers. We moved farther and farther from the pickup point.

"Perhaps we should head back?" I asked.

"We just map to the next ridge over there," she replied. "Don't worry. We'll get to the Land Rover in plenty time for pick up."

But we didn't.

I had long since eaten my juicy orange and completely drained my canteen. My dry thirst became psychologically exacerbated, much like being stuck in an elevator and suddenly feeling you need to pee. Kay took out a compass to find the shortest distance back to camp. The trek would involve going up and down multiple ridges.

We continued to walk in the blistering heat and became more and more dehydrated. Kay and I tried to chat through cracked lips while we hiked.

"When do you think we'll see the lake?"

"I bet it's over the next ridge."

"Nope, not this one."

We eventually reached the lake shore, but as thirsty as we were, could not drink the alkaline water. At camp, I gorged on squash and thought I'd never quench my thirst. And indeed, I could not. The physiology of controlling my thirst was compromised for weeks later from my close call with end-point dehydration.

From that time on, I have paid special attention to 'showing up' on time. I once submitted a conference abstract a minute before the midnight deadline - but got it in on time. I have arrived at graduate student thesis defenses and faculty meetings often a minute or two before they began - but I always showed up on time. Showing up on time shows love, respect, and courtesy to others. This behavior pays dividends in keeping social relationships intact to advancing a career. Show up on time.

North Island

The North Island's volcanic cone in the middle of Lake Turkana has served as a guidepost for the travelers in the Lake Turkana region for millennia. One day I decided to climb it and took the powerboat from our campsite to the island's only accessible black beach, surrounded by a fringe of green wild jungle hosting crocs and other wildlife.

I hiked around the dense foliage near the lake and began to climb the cone's steep slope, struggling as soft pumice cascaded out from under my feet. *"Simon and Garfunkel,"* I thought.

> *"Slip-sliding away... the nearer your destination, the more you slip slide away,"*

I glanced at my boat far below, shimmering in the heat.

"Maybe this climb wasn't such a good idea," I thought.

My mid-afternoon I reached the cone's crater plugged with black lava. I walked along its rim past fumaroles spitting out sulfur fumes and discovered a rock pyramid left behind by a prior hiker.

"*Time for a picture before I leave.*" I dropped to my knees at the base of the cairn to put my camera on top.

"*Was that movement inside?*"

I pressed my face to the rocks and peeked. A gibbon viper locked its eyes to mine and flicked its tongue an inch from my face. I flung myself backwards, my unbalanced camera clattered to the ground.

"*Deep breaths. Take deep breaths.*" And then I thought, "*The viper wants to be cool in the rocks. No threat to me.*"

I reset my camera and took a crooked photograph of a young man sporting an equally crooked grin. After sunset at camp, I came to the realization that I remained alive but for stupid luck. A cold sweat unnaturally chilled me for hours on my cot as I tried to fall sleep into the African night. "*No threat to me?*" Say what?

Deception

The National Geographic photographer, a guy named Gordon, never waited patiently to get a great photograph, but held his finger on his Nikon camera like an Uzi and took sprays of photographs, trusting one or two might be worthy of publication. A lazy version of what lots of other lazy people do with cell phones today.

Gordon seldom went into the field with us but preferred to stage 'discoveries' in the rocks behind the camp, and even set up a 'field' lab we never used but for photo-ops to show off the fossils. Most of the photographs published from the expedition were similarly staged. Gordon was a fraud, but the Leakeys had to tolerate him because his bosses paid the bills.

One week Gordon didn't return for two days after driving off by himself. We felt the dunce got lost and knew that two days in the bush without water would end him. Kay and I divvied up his cameras while Richard Leakey frantically organized an expensive search party complete with light planes from Nairobi. Another day past and then Gordon suddenly returned to camp looking hale and merry after hanging out and drinking with bored police in North Horr. If looks could kill, Richard Leakey would have gone to prison then and there.

"Where's my stuff," Gordon shouted when he entered his tent.

Kay and I returned his cameras.

"You did WHAT? Took my cameras?"

I finally had enough of Gordon when he staged Kay pretending to be fishing for the Nile perch that fed the crocs. I spotted him taking pictures of her holding a pole, its line jerked by a staffer on land, and Paul waist deep in the water rocking the boat's bow.

I got my own camera and took pictures of Gordon taking his own.

"What are you doing?"

"If I see one of your pictures of this stunt in the magazine, I'm sending my own pictures of it to your editor.

"You wouldn't."

"Try me," I said.

Gordon stalked away leaving Kay holding the line.

I walked away with the certainty I would never tolerate fraud again if I could prevent it, and I don't think I have.

Getting a Grip

Few things can lead to more emotional difficulty than being ill away from family and friends. The northern Kenyan bush provided many such opportunities: dehydration, encounters with animals or bandits, malaria from mosquitos, and giardia and dysentery from bacteria.

We traveled a day each week to draw drinking water from a wadi well surrounded by palm trees and greenery. It looked like something from "*A Thousand and One Arabian Nights*." The water tasted fine, and nobody got sick from drinking it until the day I couldn't make it even to the loo behind our tents.

To this day I have no idea what caused my full-blown dysentery. I stripped to my underpants to attempt to cool off from my fever and lay miserable on my cot. My colleagues made sure I drank plenty of squash to keep myself hydrated and gave me a spade to cover messes when I couldn't make it to the loo, more than not. I finally fell to sleep after the night cooled the air only to suddenly wake up, startled by a loud gunshot. Then another.

We had been instructed to run to our moored boat within a minute if we heard gunshots, most likely from a Somali bandit attack. In my condition, I could barely stand up, let alone run.

I uttered a kaddish for myself and a goodbye to my distant family, while clutching my field knife to my chest. *"I'll go out with a fight,"* I whispered, imagining the impossible headline:

> *"Skinny Jewish boy defends himself against African bandits with his Bowie knife."*

In my delirium, it stupidly seemed possible. I heard footsteps and cringed. Kay opened my front tent flap.

"No worries, Don. Not bandits. The male lion of the local pride wandered into camp and flicked its tail on the guard's face. He woke up and fired his Enfield to scare it off."

"Oh. Ok. Nothing to worry about. Just the local male lion walking through camp."

At breakfast when asked about the incident, Richard Leakey laughed. "If you see a lion, don't worry. It's when you *don't* see the lion, then you worry."

Words of wisdom despite what kind of lions there may be.

Eliye Springs

The National Geographic Society wanted photographs of native peoples, so one weekend Paul, Kay, Gordon, and I decided to take the boat east across the lake to the fishing town of Eliye Springs. Few people lived on the eastern side of Lake Turkana, but on its western side more gravel roads allowed for trade and larger populations.

Once we docked, we drove in the pre-arranged Land Cruiser to Lodvar, a sizeable town at the cross-roads where we found villagers tending goats and lots of thatched huts. Gordon hopped out and gave hard candies to kids running to our vehicle. For the first time in their lives, the children tasted cherry, lemon, orange, and lime and they passed the candies back and forth in delight until their elders showed up to take the treats away for themselves.

Gordon handed cigarettes to the kids who removed the paper and happily tucked the tobacco into their cheeks. All was well.

Until he started to snap photographs.

The elders became agitated. "It's ok," Gordon said as he took out a Polaroid camera, snapped a photograph of the chief, and gave him the photograph. The chief shouted angrily and handed it back.

"Sorry, I guess you don't like it," Gordon ripped the photo in half.

Villagers began to shake fists and spears at us. Kay ordered us into the vehicle while Gordon remained behind, still taking photographs.

The villagers began to close in on him.

"Get into the car or by God we'll leave you here," Paul shouted as we slowly began to move away.

Gordon finally ran and hopped in, cameras and running Africans trailing behind him.

"What was that all about? I needed those photographs," he said.

Gordon sulked all the way back to Koobi Fora where Richard said, "You did what? You showed the chief his picture and then rip it up? Don't you know tribal people think photographs capture their soul? You just ripped up the chief's soul, for Christ's sake. What response did you expect from him?"

As I said, it's worth doing a bit of research on cultures outside of your own before you visit them, even if you are a famous National Geographic Society photographer.

A Reverse Revelation

Somali tribal gangs called 'Shifta' often pillaged villages not far from where we camped near the Koobi Fora sand spit protruding into Lake Turkana. We arranged our camp tents to mimic a Kenyan military encampment. The ploy might keep the Shifta away.

Kay, the head of our team, drove our Land Rover on dry cobble stream beds to map rock outcrops and search for fossil hominids. Ahead lay arched sandstone, sandwiched layers between grey shale.

"I'm dome founded," I said.

Kay groaned at the pun. So did Gordon, for once along for the ride. We mapped geology all morning and when the afternoon sun made the rocks too hot to touch, began our trip back to the lake. Kay drove over a mogul in the gravel road and plunged our truck's back wheels deep in sand on the other side. The wheels spun uselessly.

Shifta rose to attention from their snooze under palms at a wadi in front of us.

"Get out of the truck," Kay said, "Quick. Push from the back."

"We're screwed," I replied.

She shifted the gears rapidly back and forth from first to reverse to try to get purchase while Gordon and I heaved hard on the tailgate of the Land Rover.

"Habari. Habari," Kay shouted out loudly in Swahili at the bandits; "Greetings. How are you?"

The truck jerked forward, Gordon and I dove in, and we bolted down the road, dust obscuring us from behind.

"Don't shoot," I shouted at the Somalis, who had lifted their rifles towards us.

Later at dusk after my adrenalin settled down, I rested on a ridge overlooking our camp to gaze at a sunset made crimson from volcanic dust.

Paul sat next to me.

"That sky," I said sweeping my hand left to right. "It looks like it was painted by the hand of god."

"Who?" he asked and walked away.

That moment, sitting in the cradle of human evolution, I lost my 'spiritual' faith and realized my future relies only upon my own skills, coupled with occasional blind luck, spinning wheels of opportunity gaining freedom in sand. I find the profound understanding for me still satisfying, if not completely comforting now in the last quarter of my life.

To the Moon

Neil Armstrong landed and walked on the moon that summer in Kenya when I mapped the geology where hominids had once lived. The landing occurred for us early in the morning just before the sun began to rise. Paul, Kay, and I had stayed up all night listening to BBC radio coverage of the event. A brilliant full moon hung in the sky above us when the landing occurred.

"Imagine it. One of our astronauts will walk on that before the night is over," I said, looking up.

In anticipation of the landing, we had saved a bottle of Ugandan banana gin for the event. Richard did not want to stay up with us to share the moment.

"No, I'm going to bed," he said when we invited him. "No need to listen," he said flippantly.

His decision surprised us. We never asked Richard why he thought the moon landing was not worth his time. Maybe he was just 26 years old, too young to comprehend the importance of the landing with respect to how humanity would after viewing itself in the cosmos.

Richard in public projected a bit of 'hubris' because of his skills in the African wild. Paul said if he ever got lost, the young Leakey would find him. But Richard had that hubris.

"Don, what activities did you do for fun as a teen in New York?" Richard asked me once during supper.

"I played tennis, baseball, went fishing with my friends, that kind of thing."

"Really. I trapped leopards in cages."

"Well good for you," I thought.

The prior summer, Stanley Kubrick released his movie masterpiece, '2001,' and Paul, Kay, and I talked about the film as the astronauts approached the moon, particularly the opening sequence when an ape discovers a bone femur could be used as a club, a tool. I'll never forget when the animal tossed the thing whirling into the air as it morphed into a rotating space station with the spectacular music of the Strauss's Blue Danube in the background. What an image!

There on the shores of Lake Turkana, I could easily imagine the *Homo Habilis* or the *Australopithecus* that Richard just discovered connecting our human evolution a million years ago to our human achievement in space that early July morning in 1969.

We drank the gin after Armstrong stepped on the lunar surface and made one toast after another to American technology and human ingenuity. We felt proud to be Americans and excited at the future of space technology, which in time would lead to a real space station, if not the one Kubrick envisioned in his film.

Too bad about that one.

♦ ♦ ♦ ♦ ♦ ♦

About the Author

Don Siegel was born in New York City and lived in Saratoga Springs during his childhood. He graduated with a B.S. in Geology from the University of Rhode Island. After earning his doctorate degree from the University of Minnesota in Hydrogeology (Water Geology), he joined the U.S. Geological Survey and later Syracuse University where he taught and did research until his retirement. His favorite authors are Cormac McCarthy, George Saunders, and Ernest Hemingway.

CHAPTER 7

REFLECTIONS

By Chuck Lund

The Incredible Celery Plant

Few people are aware of the incredible impact of celery in the success of our U.S. Armed Forces. Not only does celery constitute a delicious battlefield treat, but this remarkable vegetable possesses properties that had remained a secret until decorated U.S. General Hermann J. Throckmorton discovered the use of this vegetable in the defense of ancient Greek city states.

The Greek defense of Thermopylae allowed Greek democracy to survive and influence the development of democracy throughout the western world.

Few historians dispute the role of 300 heroic Spartans in delaying the advance of Persian hordes more than 2,000 years ago through the narrow canyons of Thermopylae. This delay allowed both Athenian and Spartan generals the time to mobilize both nautical and land forces and drive the Persians from the Greek lands. The subsequent survival of Greek democracy provided models of governance that have influenced the development of democracy over the centuries to the present time.

What was not known prior to general Throckmorton's discovery of the ancient Greek texts is that much of the delay of Persian forces was attributed to the tons of slippery celery stalks that lay in the path of advancing Persian forces. As described by General Throckmorton, "When those Persian guys fell all over the celery, the Spartans moved in and finished 'em off."

Celery was instrumental in the first Persian Gulf War

Celery assisted in the defeat of the Taliban following 9/11. During the First Gulf War, General Throckmorton had introduced the use of celery in tactical actions against the Iraqi soldiers retreating from the Kuwait battlefields. "We dropped tons of celery on either side of the roads back to Baghdad - we hemmed in those retreatin' varmints to a narrow slice of highway, then our jets moved in and finished 'em off."

Dick Cheney vetoed the use of celery in battles of the Second Gulf War, though he advocated its use in advanced interrogation

Prior to the U.S. invasion of Iraq in 2003, U.S. Vice President Dick Cheney disallowed use of celery by the armed forces. Citing Geneva Convention restrictions, Dick Cheney said "I realize that although the immediate routing of the Taliban in Afghanistan following 9/11 was greatly aided by celery, world opinion forced us to abandon its use by the time we invaded Iraq in 2003."

When Vice President Cheney was asked how celery might be used in the interrogation of terrorists, he declined to provide any specific methodology because of national security. He replied, "Refrigerated celery can maintain a very brittle composition for an extended period of time - you figure it out."

Death

Engulf the blasphemous grey damp struggle of your putrefaction, the incineration of deferred dreams. Leave the illusion of passivity and control for others

To Endure

Join in thought the billions of your cells already swept away in the presumed horror of extinction - allow them the same honor that you give yourself as you think about your death. Turn the energy of your desperation toward satiating the hunger of the cosmos for

Skies, Blue Eyes, Tiny Fingers Grasping Mothers Hands

Honor so-called dead elements that have given birth to billions of us from just a few, those beings now reshaped in forms committed to the delusion of self-awareness and human preeminence. Meditate on a society that chooses pigs over dogs for slaughter, cattle over dolphins, veal over horse, intelligence over instinct, nuclear devastation over chemical genocide. Imagine the power of your body dividing into trillions of parts, the agonies of those small births

Beginning Journeys to Other Forms

Pay homage to cataclysms undiscovered, pulsars borne of collapsing universes spreading once again in bursts of

Fragmentation and Creation

Above all, glorify the extinction of your consciousness, that monster creating the illusion and horror of your death, that beast glorifying the myth of individuality, the importance of one over the welfare of many, and the preeminence of concept over the

Wonders of Experience

Embrace the morphine of acceptance, the bliss of not knowing, the transcendence beyond care, the suffocation of

Desire

Grandpa

The thing about Grandpa, he could drive his '34 Ford
from Chelan to San Francisco in a day and a half.
Grandpa liked to go,

But he didn't like it when he got there.

Grandpa would buy boats and toys with real engines for
all of us grandchildren, a kid's Fantasy Land on the
edge of the Lake.
Grandpa got it all ready for us

But he didn't like it when we got there.

And you know? He could work 20 hours a day making great profits
Out of an apple orchard of twelve acres when others struggled
with a hundred. He entered into retirement wealthy,

But he didn't like it when he got there.

I tell you the guy was strong.
He could carry hundred-pound sacks under each arm
Running up steps, but he couldn't face my mother
and Grandmother about anything.
When he molested my sisters, he must have known
he'd have to face them.
When they came in to burn him with eternal rage,

He didn't like it when they got there.

When Grandpa died the whole town turned up at
The Little Stone Church he'd attended.
I'm not sure where Grandpa went when he died, but

I don't think he liked it when he got there.

Cowboy (2022)
A tiny dog with enormous virtues

Cowboy has learned many words and phrases
Walk, bed, food, treat, toy are but a few
When my wife says, "I want a foot rub," he jumps off
Her lap and heads for his pillow bed,
Understanding that mommy's lap
Will be unavailable during her foot rub by Dad.
"Shouldn't that dog be on a leash?"
I respond, "He's on a voice leash,"
He freezes when he hears "Wait for Daddy."
He walks calmly past other dogs and humans when I point and speak
"Right here, right here."
He heads for the trash bin when I say "Let's dump the trash"
For the mailbox when I say, "Let's get the mail,"
And for the bedroom when we say, "Let's go to bed."
He twirls with joy when I say
"Time to feed the puppy," or
"Let's go see Mommy."

He yips at my wife at 7:00 pm - time for her
to go to bed with him and read
He stretches, stares at us and woofs politely
When he asks to go outside

He displays propensity for fierce combat
When he is on a leash protecting Momma, and
When he is warning those ringing our doorbell,
All with the braying of a massive beast.

Although this may all seem banal to outside observers,
the above traits have endeared Cowboy to us over the years.

Maxie (1998)

My dog Max, a very old soul,
body crippled, spirit whole.
He shares his peace and loyalty,
a pat on the head, his ecstasy.

Enormous size, very small temper,
often in pain, nary a whimper.
Small children ask, "Can Max come play?"
pulling his jowls, making him lay.

Terrible odor, Zen-like peace,
once-a-year shave, beloved fleece.
He woofs when he thinks I'm going somewhere,
a gentle reminder, a wish to be there.

Fearsome to strangers, angry toward none,
timeless patience, his life nearly done.
I touch him and hold him whenever I can.
Newfoundland essence, a great gift to man.

Maxie (1999)

My dog's crippled leg-
How much longer can he go on?
I rationalize that the success of his life
is now achieved in length of years and
by all other measures, after all, he continues
to radiate peace as he struggles to rise
and bestow slobbered respects.

Not fat at 150 pounds,

he asks for help with a mild bark,

help to get him up on the porch even though

his neck chain I pull causes him to choke - he coughs

his adoration and thanks for his ability to

look at us through the kitchen window once more.

He does not deserve to die. His grace and good nature create no requirements for worry or guarded approach, a gift rare among humans and uncommon even among dogs.

I am not ready for his death -

I am far more ready for my own.

A Dying Wish by Anonymous as told to Charles Lund

Last week I found out I will be dead within a month. They caught it in a blood test - a rare form of cancer that exhibits symptoms only in life's final moments. The prognosis is based on observation of the sheaths of death cells surrounding every body system - rare, but not rare enough to escape the record of how and when someone dies from this.

"We didn't want to share this with you until we were certain." They showed me the raft of second opinions to document the finding.

So I've said to myself - glad to know it won't be painful, but, maybe better not to have known. As I thought later, the difference between a forewarned execution and an assassination. There seems to be no DNR or Living Will choice for knowing or not knowing such a narrow alternative. And how would the doctors present this option, even to themselves, "Would you like to know if you're dying, or not?" The irony of such a choice, when presented with said choice, the cat would be out of the bag, thus nullifying its value in the first place. Also, there seems to be no way of incorporating this into any power of attorney.

Another irony is - I feel bad about not feeling bad. This kind of ironic double-backing has been a constant in my life, leading to the quest in the philosophical or psychological literature for explanation. The only explanation that makes reasonable sense is from sociology - I have sociopathic tendencies. In truth, feeling bad about not feeling bad is only fleeting - most of the time I don't feel bad at all.

So, this final test of personality, should I reveal this condition to anyone? My lifelong friend in Europe? Nah, he and I communicate once a year. For months he ignored an email with the subject "death" because he thought it was a notice of my death - when it was actually a poem about death. By this action I assume he would not care to hear about my death, impending or not.

To my blood relatives? Nah. My death may or may not be a relief to them. But I don't want to ascertain whether their expressed grief is genuine. I think most feel I'm a boastful pain in the ass, despite my occasional sense of humor. I don't really know, and don't care, and I feel bad about not feeling bad, as if I'm imputing to them some of my own tendency to not care about much of anything, or anyone.

Everyone else, extended family, casual acquaintances, my wife and others perceive me as one who wants to stand out too much, too goal oriented, too dismissive. I can't help but think at least some of them would parrot the old country western tune "Thank god and greyhound he's gone." I'm ok with this, but maybe I shouldn't be ok about not caring what they would feel about it.

My last and only wish is that I will keep this "not bad" feeling until the end. I'm certainly not going to ask anyone whether they want to know if I'm dying, or not. I might, but probably wouldn't, feel bad about their answer - or, in the refutation to this whole argument, I might be afraid of *anything* they would answer.

Time

If I, by salvation or passive destiny, remain beyond time
what time will there be for remembered time - wisps of lovers,
children growing, times of joy and sorrow?

When am I to nurture memories of precious times-
In a time beyond time?
Where shall I sit to remember-
In a world without end, amen?

To what End does Eternity stretch its noble definition,
Its warm Comforting Certainties that defy Comprehension?

Oh blessed boundaries that I know
The outline of loved ones,
Boundaries of lips, eyes, conversations, glances,
Taking time to be here or there.

Love and marriage,
Time and space,
Death and taxes,
Human race.

The Edge of the Universe,
the end of my nose,
The End of Time,
the end of me.

My Dead Father Shows up in My Dreams (With Little Notice or Intent)

Mostly a brittle and
Intimidating Presence
That I often take to task
By screaming or
Tearing off his limbs

When he was alive, I became
Physically stronger than he, but
I had little conviction or self-esteem
To challenge him,
Even with my words

In the dreams I occasionally
Try to impress him,
But the interaction devolves
Into my annihilation
Of his spectral form

I'm not sure whether my
Behavior in my dreams is some kind of
Recompense for his parental
Brutality and disparagements
Toward me during his life.
My thoughts toward him
In my conscious hours
Are much kinder, and I'm not
Sure why. I cannot claim altruistic motives,

Ingrained in these daytime thoughts are two basic images.
One is of him as a four-year-old boy looking fearful
and forlorn next to a giant horse.
The other is his ghost I have
Summoned from the grave to ask
Whether he would return to this earth
He breaks down crying with the
Anguish of an unforgiven soul

My Father died after writing
Apologies to me and my sisters
For his harsh punishments and
Demands for achievement, and for his life as a
"Cripple who was raised by Cripples."

Over the years I have recounted
The ways I have failed my own children
Fortunately, a remarkable woman has
Instilled in me better behaviors as a father,
A redemptive, albeit imperfect, foundation
For our children and future generations.

Those People at the Office

I'm not sure where they all get their purpose, or even what their
Purpose is; they and their purposes are like so many grey bats
floating around, not looking at me, but sensing that
I drift with them, without purpose, surely not their purpose

I smile when I can and bury myself in the redemption of
activity, looking up occasionally to wonder at their activity,
their sidelong glances not reading me, god I hope not,
I gotta have this job, smile once more at them, they may be bats, but
They can't sense everything, can they?

Shut the door, that's it, and if I do come out make
sure the stuff from her gets to the place over there by him,
and make sure they know, without their knowing I intended
their knowing, that I did that as a great favor - which should
buy some more time if it is ever discovered that
I do not share their purpose, whatever that is!

While I am waiting for the revelation of purpose, I make the
Coffee when it's my turn, laugh at a joke, share one of my own,
try not to draw attention, flatter the boss even if it's true ... never
say anything that will cause a frown or create incomprehension
... turn in high numbers, but not too high ... volunteer for the
Xmas committee...save aggression for small enemies or for the
defense of fellow workers...collect the paycheck ... make it
through the weekend without colliding too hard with Monday ...
grieve only in private for the dismissed colleague - - -
Gotta quit typing .... another bat's cruising by.

Missing

If I hid from you, would you miss me?
How long would it take you to miss me?
How painful a missing would that missing be,
That missing of yours for the missing of me?

If I hid out of sight, would I miss you?
Would separateness cause me to miss you?
If I hid round the block in a room with no lock,
How long could I stay 'fore I missed you?

If I never came back, would you miss me?
Would it take such a missing to miss me?
Proof of no breath? Affidavit of death?
If that's what I gave, would you miss me?

When I'm with you, you often go missing.
You're off somewhere else when we're kissing.
Sometimes when we talk, your mind takes a walk,
You nod, but I know you're not listening.

If I never came back, WHO would miss me?
No one to love me or diss me?
Out of sight, out of mind, just a matter of time,
Before EVERYONE would not miss me.

So please one more time, just kiss me.
Not your soul, not your mind, just kiss me.
Tonight I may go, where I'd never know
Whether you and the world wouldn't miss me

The Gambist

She lives! Not a painting,
But a vision unreal nevertheless.
She sits but three feet away, yet of
another time, ever absorbed in her
tender caress of the wooden instrument
that cares naught but to fulfill projection
of her elegance and union with ancient centuries.

I cannot but stare at the cultivation of unbundled
curls falling across frail limbs, all to nurture
phrases toward ephemeral fulfillment. Her
bow glides toward lilting denouements as
tapered as her waist, recalling eras of
deflected passion, restrained Eros.

She pauses with classic features pursed,
waiting as I and fellow musicians
promenade toward entrances
as unobtrusive as endings
she has played before.
She begins again with push of strings and swelling
of sound that reveals no purpose other
than ascetic simplicity.

I wonder at this apparition that
has been so produced for our
awareness, skin white and
ghostly wan, body of grace
inspiring contemplation
of tone and form
long buried.

Empathy

My wife says, "You've never lost someone you truly loved." I say "What about Zekie? I still grieve for him." She says, "He wasn't a someone, he was a dog." She's right, my sorrow for anyone's passing has mostly been a

Twinge

Perhaps slightly more for my dad, stepson and our friend Susie. I've been accused by others of having sociopathic tendencies - In my mind perhaps the same degree to which a therapist once told

Me

"You have a bit of ambiguity about your sexual orientation." Then, the other night I saw my wife sleeping, propped up, mouth

Agape

Reminding me of some I'd transported as an ambulance driver "That's it." I thought. My horror at the possibility of her death hit Me with the realization of what might lie behind humankind's

Obsession With Death

Philosophical truth be damned, existential angst is a cover
For the truth of loss that is rooted mainly in our conscious

Existence

A loss that is personal, a loss that transcends any collective
Bullshit angst dreamed up by social science practitioners.
Kohlberg's levels of morality aside, while I may not be on top of
His spectrum of moral development, I am sure that my
Pain at my wife's passing would be a lot more than the loss of
Personal comfort. Even so, I rarely experience

Pain at Humanity's Collective Loss.

Serenity

*"I do not fear death. I had been dead
billions and billions of years before I was born,
and had not suffered the slightest
inconvenience from it."* Mark Twain

I once asked my ten year old son
"What do you think happens when we die?"

He replied

"It will be just like before we were born."
I'm not sure where he got this,
As I don't remember sharing this view with him.

A Jewish acquaintance told me
That all her children had died.
I asked her if she felt anguish.

She replied

"I have no grief - they had their gift."

I've had many views of death throughout

My life

From fundamentalist Christian
Views of Heaven or Hell
To beliefs including reincarnation,
Universal consciousness and
An oblivion that renders life

Meaningless

Now in my 74th year,

I am happier

Than at any time of my life.

I've learned mental habits that

Stave off fear

I'm taking anti-aging supplements and have

resurrected an old hobby to train and

Compete in Powerlifting Competitions

Nevertheless, I know that I am

Dying

Memory is slowly

Decaying

Body parts and functions are

Inexorably

Winding Down

Patience with the struggles between

Expectations and reality is

Wearing Thin

Whatever months, years or decades are left to me

I see

Death

as an increasingly

Important partner

That comforts me with the

Promise of total serenity

Redemption

Messages of despair
Seep out from the media like
Invisible poison
Death, starvation
Homelessness, millions
Flung from their jobs and homes
Onto the mercies of an uncertain future

The worldwide COVID pandemic
Now ravages all societies

Our family's donations to the poor
As meager as they've been, now amount to
Gut-wrenching Insignificance,
Even more pitiful given
The millions of newly impoverished
In our own country

I feel crushed and helpless
No amount of intellectual sophistry
Can allay this feeling

The COVID virus
Slays innocent victims en masse
We can see individual victims on
24-hour news if we choose

It's not unlike images of horror in the
Slaughter of baby seals,
Or the terror of those facing
Nazi execution squads
I shut out the crushing reality of all this
By seeking redemption for the
Acts in my life that have
Demonstrated anger, intolerance
Hateful words and actions

The horrors of this time
Drive me to a commitment of
Treating people with
Compassion and respect
To discontinue habits that
Scorn or deride others

I can no longer conjure my own
World views or philosophies.
I don't know what a world-wide healing
Or salvation would ever mean

Despite never achieving this perfectly,
What I can strive for is my own redemption
Through good thoughts and behavior toward others

A
Memory of
My Third Christmas

HOBBLED HORSE...NIGHT-CLAD LAD

WITH LIGHTS....................WITH TREE

ON SNOW..............................AND DAD

AND CAR..................................A SENSE

LIGHTS GLOW................................A TASTE

WITH MAGIC...................................REMAINING

FIFTY YEARS

NOW LOST

THE BOOK

WHOSE PICTURES

MADE THE

SCENES I

TOOK INTO

MY SOUL

THAT DOES

NOT LOOK

BEYOND THE

CORTEX THRILL

OF MIND

THAT KEEPS

THOSE MAGIC

SCENES STILL

MINE

The Hun Named Attila

Said the wives of the Hun named Attila,
"You no longer give us a Thrilla.
You sit round all day,
You got nothing to say.
You look and smell like a Gorilla."

Said the sons of the Hun named Attila,
"We know you're not over the Hilla.
Please take no offense,
Don't mount your defense.
Just do your best if you Willa."

Said the daughters of the Hun named Attila.
"It would help if you just took your Pilla.
Please shower and shave,
And try to behave
Otherwise you are going to look Silla."

Attila had no other Skilla,
But to plunder and torture and Killa.
He said...... "If I had my way,
I'd make those wives pay,
And rip them apart like Godzilla."

But I cannot harm my dear Jilla.
Nor Dorothy nor Rose nor Priscilla
If I tore them apart,
It would near break my heart.
So,,,,,, I'm gonna lay back and just Chilla."

He said - "there is a bad wife I could Killa.
That ornery old wife named Cruella.
I gave her that name,
'Cause she drove me insane,
I banished her far from this Villa."

The Corner of the Living Room

The Corner's simplicity
Invites relief from
Cluttered thoughts

The Corner's sharp edge
Protects me from
Imagined hardships,

The Corner's carpet
Soothes away
Angry turmoil

I often imagine
Dwelling in that Corner -
Invisible from the scrutiny and
Judgement of Others

♦ ♦ ♦ ♦ ♦

About the Author

Charles (Chuck) Lund and his wife Ilona relocated to Silver Spring, Maryland four years ago to be close to their young grandchildren. In Leisure World they enjoy many of the community's activities. Chuck's background includes management in Healthcare, Corrections, and Fine Arts. Ilona's background is in Healthcare and Education. They both love history, art, and music.

CHAPTER 8

MEMORIES, THOUGHTS, AND FEELINGS

By Joanie Friedlander

First Date

My First Date came from a tree. I ate it.

Nature Walks

My neighbor Lynne and I walk every morning around Leisure World and see many beautiful flowers and colorful bushes, trees of all kinds, and nature's animals, birds, and butterflies.

One day we saw a butterfly on the golf course and while we were watching, another butterfly came by. They passed each other, then for quite a while, they seemed to be dancing together. How romantic!

Often we see deer. Once, as we sat on a wide tree stump, a doe came to the small tree in front of us and began nibbling on its leaves. Then next thing we knew, she stood up on her hind legs, and pulled a branch down with her mouth as she continued to eat more leaves. That's the first time I saw that!

As we watched, she got back down on her four legs. With her big beautiful brown eyes she watched us for a while as we smiled at her. Then the delightful doe turned and trotted to the trees that line the stream; her white tail seemed to wave goodbye.

Another time, way behind Lynne's home, in the park-like setting, we saw four deer laying under a shady tree. We watched them for a while, before continuing on our walk. Those deer were there the next day, too; and the day after that!

About a week later in the same area, we saw three does standing and we stopped to watch. To the right of us, we saw a young buck approaching. "Go to your family," Lynne directed him. He was very young because his antlers were just a bit more than buds. He joined the rest of the deer as Lynne advised.

We always see birds, including many robins. Leisure World seems packed with sparrows, and chickadees, as well as ever-present crows. Squirrels are often in our path, or there are two chasing each other up a tree. Once in a while we see a cute chipmunk.

Often, we spot Mourning Doves and sometimes male and female Cardinals, and Blue Jays.

Twice we saw a beautiful all-red bird called a Summer Tanager. One time a Summer Tanager was in a tree and a Blue Jay landed on the same tree. Then the Blue Jay flew to another tree, chased by the Summer Tanager. Again the Blue Jay flew away, followed closely by the Summer Tanager. I wonder what they were trying to do with each other!

On the subject of birds, we were in my husband Dan's car when he spotted a Pileated Woodpecker! Being an avid birdwatcher, he turned the car around and we parked near the tree the woodpecker was in. We watched the fabulous bird for quite a while. It was quite a treat!

Returning to deer, as I walked on my way to Lynne's home, I saw a very young spotted fawn. I watched her, without getting too close, as she walked behind a bush.

Another day, Lynne and I saw a deer family with a buck, doe, and fawn who still had his spots. I had my camera with me, but before I could take more than one photograph, the deer suddenly raced away, across the street to the golf course (I guess I scared them).

Before COVID began, I used to walk behind my house beyond the little stream where there were, for a month or more, five deer. Two does would be laying comfortably, while three young spotted fawns walked around close to their mothers. Occasionally, one or two of the fawns would lay down by their moms.

At times the five deer would be walking near the little stream, and back again. I used to think of them as "my deer." I would take a walk every day just to visit with them. I didn't take any pictures and they seemed to watch me and not be afraid. That was so fun! I'm glad all the deer are back again this year.

The Fall Season

Red, yellow, green, and brown

Colorful leaves upon the ground

Squirrels scampering, bunnies hopping, birds chirping all around

We're in Playland as my friend puts and yes, I do feel grand

All the trees now in their splendor

We walk, talk, and enjoy the bright sunshine, these crisp fall days

Neighbors with their dog or dogs, jogging, or just out for their
    morning constitutional

Papa deer relaxing under a pine tree while Mama deer and yearlings
    eat their breakfast of grass and leaves

What happened to Summer - Seasons sure change fast

My Dan's Autumn has come at last.

Winter Wonderland Adventures

My sweetheart Dan is now my loving husband. He is a real outdoor buff. Nearly every day in all weather, he jogs in a nearby park or in his neighborhood. Each October until he was in his late 60's Dan entered the Marine Corps Marathon (26.2 miles) to raise money for fighting cancer. My sweet and generous Dan, now 77 years old, still runs each year to raise money for good causes. Currently he runs in "Ben's Run" to fight Childhood Cancer and the Marine Corp 10K to raise money to fight cancer for the Leukemia and Lymphoma Society.

Dan started running over three decades ago to train for mountain climbing in the United States. But I'm getting ahead of myself. It all began when Dan was 15 years old and he read the fascinating story of Mallory and Irvine; and their climb up Mount Everest.

Inspired by those brave souls, Dan took up climbing. Once, he and his niece Claire realized their dream by joining a safari in Africa to see and photograph the wild animals, and to climb a mountain.

In fact 29 years ago, Dan climbed to the top of "Longs Peak" in the Rocky Mountain National Park Wilderness. The mountain is among the highest at 14,255 feet in the United States. Over a hundred people have died trying to summit the mountain. It is a demanding climb, but my strong and determined husband did it successfully!

In the winter, Dan goes cross-country skiing. One snowy winter's day he was cross country skiing on the sidewalks in his neighborhood when he saw another skier cross-country skiing on the sidewalk! They met for the first time and became good friends who have traveled to New Hampshire together for many cross-country ski trips and even overseas on one occasion.

Dan always wanted to drive a dogsled in Alaska since he read John London's "Call of the Wild" in high school. He has participated in five dogsledding trips. The first dogsledding trip was in Maine. Once he even pulled the sled of a dogsled team instead of leading from behind. What a Winter Adventure that was.

At last, the day came to fulfill his longtime dream by dogsledding in Alaska. While there he even saw those amazing Northern Lights, the Aurora Borealis. His Winter Wonderland Adventure!

As for me, I love walking in fluffy snow (I used to try and catch a snowflake on my tongue). I love watching the snow falling outside my window. It looks just like a snow globe! And I love getting up the next day and seeing a brand new blanket of pure white snow covering all the grass and upon the rooftops and trees.

I delight in how new bright snow sparkles and makes the whole world look like a pristine Winter Wonderland from my passenger seat window in the car, shuttle bus, or bus. Out in the freshly fallen snow, it's so much fun packing the snow into snowballs and throwing them where they won't hurt anyone. I still love lying down in my winter coat and flapping my wings to create a snow angel. And of course, I have to make a snowman!

Once, when my daughter Jill was not much more than a toddler, I created an oil painting called, "A Child's Winter." The snowman we made together is in the painting; and in the front is a happy and playful little Jill in her red snowsuit. She is having the time of her life climbing in the middle of the fluffy snow covered tree in the front lawn of our house. In my painting, the wind whips the snow around dangerously within the bare branches of a tall tree (to show the side of winter learned when I became an adult).

My husband Dan embraces winter with a childlike delight because he is known to "conquer" both of his passions, cross-country skiing and jogging. Through Dan's detailed diaries, I am able to enjoy with him his mountain climbing, hiking, and dogsledding vacations.

Growing up, and as a teenager, I always enjoyed sledding, skating, and building a snowman here and there. As a child, I loved building snow forts and snow castles; and even snow caves. Once as a young mother, my daughter Jill helped me build an entire snow family.

I made a Snow Bunny for Baby Jill one very snowy Easter when we lived in Cedar Rapids, Iowa. Astonishing, how fine! Just for the two of us: our own Winter Wonderland in springtime!

Once There Was an Accident

One Metro train ran into another causing an accident on the Red Line I took to and from work. Normally, no one speaks to anyone during their ride on a train; however, after the accident the passengers began talking to each other.

A few days later, I was coming home from work on the Red Line when a handsome man caught my eye and we smiled at each other, sparks flew both ways - this was, as the song says, "Some Enchanted Evening." On the crowded train we were standing as all the seats were taken. When the train stopped and we heard the announcer's familiar voice, "We will be moving momentarily." Both he and I were looking at each other and said "momentarily" along with the voice.

Day after day, we would see each other and whoever got a seat first would save a place for the other. We introduced ourselves and to my surprise and delight he would create "observations" in limerick form to share with me during the train ride.

I brought my sketchpad and began sketching other passengers and when he saw them, he wrote a clever observation about my sketches to paste into my sketchbook.

We began to date about a year after we met and saw each other at least once a week for 11 years. After I retired and wasn't riding the train anymore, we continued dating. Then COVID came to town, he decided to call me each morning to make sure I was okay.

After one year of those early morning calls, on Mother's Day, 2020 he came to my house with flowers, chocolate, and ice cream to ask for my hand in marriage. I was speechless for the first time in my life - I was beside myself with joy - but before I had a chance to respond he was out of my house to the store.

Immediately, I called him to say, "Yes, Yes, a thousand times Yes!"

Today is our wedding day!!! His name is Dan and he is my Man!!!

We are both so happy and so are our families.

Once there was an accident and we lived happily ever after.

It Was a Dark and Stormy Night

It was a dark and stormy night. The evening before, I had dinner with my friends and after a long and busy day, I was wiped out. Anxious to get my shoes (and bra) off - and into my PJs, I placed the plastic bag of leftovers on my bedside table so I could "get horizontal" (as my sweet husband phrases it).

Yes, it was a dark and stormy night but here, I was cozy in my bed for just a second or two. Before I knew, I had dozed off. I do not know how long I slept.

Then I looked to see the time and noticed my bag of leftovers still sitting where I left it. I picked up the bag to take to the fridge.

I did not turn on any lights because the ambient light was bright enough to see my way to the kitchen. But now, as I turned to return to my bedroom a shadowy figure appeared right in front of me, blocking my way.

My heart was beating out of my chest, I swear I could even hear it. I don't remember being so scared. How did he get in?

"Hello? Hello?" No answer. I moved, he moved. I know I locked the door, didn't I? My mind was racing for answers.

"Hello?" I frantically asked, still no response.

Little by little as my eyes adjusted to the dark and almost laughing at how silly I was ... could it be? I noticed the hall closet to the left; to check my perception I put my right hand through the shadow - and gratefully touched the wall behind it (or at least that's how it looked to me at the time).

Relieved, I realized my eyes had been reacting to the sudden and bright light in the refrigerator (when I opened it), in the similar way flash photography used to "blind" us for a second or two. We used to say, "Now I'm seeing spots in front of my eyes."

Home safe and all is well. This time I fell asleep for the night to the soothing sound of rain falling, for the worst of the storm had passed.

And as I drifted off to sleep, I imagined there would be a beautiful rainbow in the sky early the next morning, especially for me. I will be with my new husband. The two of us are over the rainbow in a love that will last forever.

The Blue Straw Hat

My next-door neighbor Lynne and I were taking our first walk after my honeymoon in Pennsylvania where we had three days of sunny weather.

As we began our walk, Lynne asked me how my new husband and I dealt with all the rain; because those same three days it rained every day in Maryland. She was happy for me that the weather was good in Silver Spring for our wedding ceremony, the reception, the car ride to Pennsylvania, our vacation there, and on the way back.

To keep the sun out of our eyes, both Lynne and I sometimes wear wide brimmed hats. That day, we enjoyed walking and talking. In fact, the walk was very refreshing, having missed walking with her each morning since I left. We walked up the lane, out of the park in our backyards, and made a left to go on the sidewalk; a route we often take.

Suddenly a gust of wind hit us and Lynne's blue straw hat literally flew off and blew away; it rolled down the sidewalk, past where we exited the park. It rolled on its edge (and I was reminded of the song "On Top of Spaghetti"). Just as Lynne bent down to pick it up: woosh, the wind took it again! This time her blue straw hat flew (looking so much like a flying saucer) all the way across the street.

Lynne went running after her hat. Checking both ways for traffic, Lynne crossed the street. I stayed and prayed the hat wouldn't move again. I hoped she would not lose it. Fortunately, it hit a curb and stopped in less than a minute before Lynne caught up to it. She picked it up and put it back on her head, and we both smiled. Then she carefully crossed the road back to where I was waiting for her. Wouldn't you know it, just as we caught our breath, my own hat flew off! What a comedy of errors.

The brim of my straw colored hat is floppy, so it stayed put for me to pick up and to put back on my head where it belonged. The rest of the way home, however, we held our hands up to hold our hats when we felt a breeze speeding towards us.

We reached my house and Lynne came in for a few card games. It wasn't until the next morning I realized right there on my end table was Lynne's Blue (Famous Flying Saucer) Straw Hat!

One Sunny Day

"What a nice sunny day," I thought to myself. Lynne and Mary are our neighbors. I'm on my way to meet Lynne for our morning walk. Two Blue Jays were flying ahead of me. One goes to a branch of a high tree while the other lands on the roof to my right. Spring is almost here and I can feel the change of seasons in the air. All around us the birds are chirping, squirrels are scampering, and when I look closely on the branches of trees, I'm starting to see little green buds.

There is a Robin, then another, and a third. It is often said seeing a Robin is a sure sign of spring. We have our coats on this morning, although we do not need them in the afternoon. Spring is trying to spring to life in front of our eyes. As Lynne says, "We're all in anxious anticipation for it to be here." On our walk yesterday, we saw yellow daffodils lift their sunny heads to welcome the warmer weather. In the distance, we see three pink trees, a little rosier in color than the Cherry Blossom trees. Today, the sky is a lovely light blue with fluffy white clouds. The grass is well-tended and very green.

American flags proudly wave in front and in back of our neighbors' houses in the slight breeze. It's good to be an American; alive and able to take walks in the beautiful park-like area behind our homes. Soon the yellows, light-greens, and other pastel colors will brighten all the bushes and trees; while flowers join the awakening of spring. There's a tree with white blossoms!

People are walking their dogs who trot along in front, besides, or behind them. We stop to say hello and sometimes pet their dogs. We wave and say hi to others who are also taking in the sunshine on this very pleasant day.

In my husband Dan's backyard, four deer comfortably relax and nibble on the grass. Two hawks were there yesterday and today only one. A female Cardinal is a great treat for Dan to see, as well as all the beautiful birds.

137

While I was at my table reading in front of my closed-in porch, I spotted a male Cardinal on the bush closest to my house. I got up to watch him until he flew away. Tonight is Mary's night as we celebrate her birthday with good friends and a fun dinner at one of our favorite restaurants. And thanks to the joy on Mary's face and in our hearts, my sunny day is lasting long into the night.

Our Unexpected Snowstorm

It's around 2:00 in the afternoon on Saturday. I'm relaxing on the living room sofa with my book and coffee. Looking out of the large window of my enclosed patio the snow-lined trees look magnificent even the ones with the little buds beginning to turn green. And the bushes the red Cardinal had hopped on yesterday are now blanketed with snow.

I lay down my book to warm my hands on my coffee mug I bought when I retired. As I take another sip and read the saying on its side, "Goodbye Tension, Hello Pension."

Suddenly a strong gust of wind outside causes the tree branches to wave wildly and I notice snow on the rooftops being blown off. It was so warm yesterday, I can still see the parking lot's blacktop. No snow has accumulated there.

Oh my! Now snow is coming from the sky with a vengeance, flying to the right, now to the left, then to the right again. There are no squirrels or birds out today but the hatted neighbor on the other side of our parking lot needs to go somewhere. With a long handled brush, he swiftly cleans the snow away from the front window of his car. Then he moves to the back, and to the other side. Good, it comes off easily, no scraping required. Then with his gloved hands, he brushes off his coat, opens his car door and puts his brush away. Soon he gets in his car, backs out, goes to my left, and I don't see him anymore.

Meanwhile, our unexpected snowstorm rages on. I watch a while then return to reading my book. When I look up again, there seems to be fewer snowflakes and the wind is almost calm. Tonight, we "Spring Forward" with our clocks. While yesterday really did feel like spring, today seems to be a return of winter and I wonder what the weather will be like tomorrow.

As much as we think we can, and many have tried throughout the ages, no one can change the weather. While weather predictions have improved over the years, decades, centuries; we are still learning. A good example is the dire prediction of heavy thunderstorms for the morning and day of my wedding this past August. However, sunshine won out with not a hint of rain at all. What a comfortable and perfect day for me and Dan, and our guests.

Springtime Shuttle Ride

With my rolling cart, I walk up the ramp of the Shuttle

And I say Hi to our friendly driver who waits 'till I take a seat

Then we're on our way. I look out the window and what do I see

Lacey cherry blossoms blooming so joyfully in front of dark green pines

A man walking his German Shepherd on the sidewalk looking very happy.

Here and there daffodils of bright and pale yellows

Deep pink and purple flowers and pansies dot area signs and lawns

In front of a home and sitting together are statues of a doe and a fawn

Next to the door, their dog statue just happens to also be a German Shepherd!

In Spring and always, our Shuttles carry us along anywhere we need to be

And when I take the Shuttle to see these things, I too am very happy.

The First Hat

Perhaps the first hat ever invented was to keep the owner's head warm.

Many decades ago, right after college, I bought an elegant gray hat with a large feather just because it was such fun. I kept it, but never had an occasion to wear it. I was disappointed it was lost in my move from New Jersey to Maryland. For it was the first hat I bought on my own.

A few years after I moved to Leisure World in the late 1990s, I began a collection of hats. What is it with me and hats? Hmmm. I had one hat, then seven, and now seventeen hats! To paraphrase a song, "I don't know why I love them, but I do."

My fascination with hats began when I joined the Red Hat Society club where all members were supposed to wear a red hat with a purple scarf (unless they were under 50 years old where they would wear a pink hat with a lavender scarf). I went to a thrift shop and bought my first red hat.

Later three friends gifted me with several wonderful red hats, a springtime one, a western one, and a winter one. One cold frosty day, my friend gave me a woolen hat with an attached scarf. Later I bought a fancier one with fake fur.

My daughter sent me a baseball cap of our home team (the New York Mets). And when I moved here, my husband Dan took me to a Nationals game where he bought me a Nat's baseball cap.

On a vacation trip to Branson, at the urging of my friend, I bought a souvenir cap with red sparkles. And during my vacation to the Grand Canyon I purchased a pink (I'm a kid at heart) hat that says "Grand Canyon."

On another vacation I bought a wide brimmed, straw-colored hat with a colorful turquoise and orange hatband. Two more red hats purchased from my local gift shop back at home. One I added a scarf to, and one just in case my coat's hood blows off. And one more black hat that I think "looks cute" on me.

My next hat was an investment to keep my head dry in the case of rain: a waterproof one. Dan gifted me a baseball hat celebrating the Chicago Symphony Orchestra. I was born in Chicago, and our niece lives there.

The last hat I received is also one Dan gave me - a nice deep blue woolen hat that's works very well to keep my head warm.

Wandering Thoughts

There was a time I felt lucky after leaving my group of friends to go home by flight instead of by car.

It was amazing; when I went somewhere (every aspect of my life - home, school, work, playground, neighborhoods) existed on floating islands (like puffy clouds in the blue sky). On a sunny day, by taking long strides, I would actually fastwalk in the air/(fly) up or down, to wherever I wanted to go. I experienced this night after night, in my dreams of course.

What a handy mode of transportation that would be in real life, if it could happen. (Is that what "jetpacks" were invented for?)

- - - - - - - - - -

And what of the time I looked for my glasses, here and there and everywhere. "Maybe they're in the bathroom," I thought and when I got there, I looked in the mirror. I had them on. I had been looking through them!

- - - - - - - - - -

Tonight, I decided to make a pot of coffee before going to bed, for the next morning. I got it all ready and plugged it in; then read my book and got ready for bed before checking on the coffee to turn it off before retiring for the evening.

- - - - - - - - - -

Thinking way back, I remember a very hectic day in my life when my daughter Jill was little and she had her friends over for a pajama party. The next morning all the kids were up and I made them breakfast. I looked at the coffee pot then realized it had been on the whole night.

Relieved there was still enough coffee left in the pot from the night before to keep it from catching on fire. I was totally delighted to help myself to a cup of hot beverage to jump-start my day.

- - - - - - - - - -

Okay, getting back to the coffee for tomorrow, I go to turn it off and whoops! There is no coffee in the pot. Oh shucks, will I have to buy a new coffee pot again? Let's see, yes it's plugged in. Yes, uh oh, I forgot to turn it on! So I did and let the coffee brew and eventually I came back to turn it off so it will be ready the next morning.

And decades later, with the magic of a microwave (an invention unbeknownst to me when Jill was little) I can enjoy a delicious cup of steaming coffee to start my day. (Yes, I know about coffeepots with timers and a Keurig that brews one cup at a time. I don't have, nor do I wish to buy either one).

- - - - - - - - - -

"The point is to make the people happy, not show off your skill." That's what he said to me after the little boy and his mother went away in a huff. You see, I was sketching portraits (on the Boardwalk in Atlantic City, before there were Casinos) and the mother was so angry, insisting my charcoal drawing of her son looked nothing like him. She had shouted her opinion to my manager. He looked back and forth from my sketch to her son and answered that yes, he did think the picture looked like the little boy. I learned that day people see what they want to see and our job as artists is to draw a better version (similar but better or more perfect) than what's in front of us to make people smile.

My favorite sketch was one of a man who didn't have the money to pay for it so I gave it to him (the manager was really mad at me for doing that). One of the artists there sketched me and I still have the charcoal sketch on the wall in my dining room.

In the privacy of my home, I would paint what I felt and those paintings reflected my innermost feelings and emotions as well as the subject in front of me, or in my mind. It was very therapeutic and helped me live through the traumatic first marriage I had with my ex.

In addition, I made commissioned pastels of still life's flowers, trees or much-loved toys, cats, kittens, puppies, or other pets. I also made pastel paintings of members of their families to give away to coworkers and to friends and relatives. My most memorable one was the closeup pastel painting of a bride sitting by the window with her fancy lace bordering her sheer wedding veil.

I love to sketch and paint; I also love to write. Being creative and writing or doing any kind of art always makes me happy. It's also enjoyable to share my work so others can smile with me.

Car Excitement

I love the little gold car my daughter, Jill, gave me because it gets me and my friends to most of the places we like to go.

When I was in high school, driving a car for me (going fast with the music as loud as possible) was my way of relaxing. It was Mom's red Ford that my sister, Merrily, and I drove. One day, Merrily and I were in the car when it was very low on gas. We stopped at the station and found that we had only 35 cents between us. That turned out to be enough money to buy the gas we needed to get to where we were going and home again!

Designing a car was my assignment in my high school mechanical drawing class. My entry was a streamlined car, similar to the Corvette (I didn't know that when I created my design). It was not until I drove Mom's Ford in the snow I realized the slanted back window that was so sleek and aerodynamic (like the car I designed), collected snow making it difficult to see behind in bad weather.

Tommy, the boy I met at work and married, then eventually had to divorce, impressed me with his convertible. It was Girl Scout "forest green" with striking white racing stripes and a white interior. The canvas top was also a bright white. It was equipped with a huge "454" engine, he always bragged about. When we were dating, he picked me up and we went to work together. When I landed a job in a different place, Tommy bought me the first car I ever owned - it was a used, ugly, boxy-shaped vehicle. It did get me to work and back. The next year, and each time after that, when Tommy bought a convertible for

143

himself, he bought me the hard-topped version of the identical car; beautiful Malibu's.

One winter, on a curvy and icy hill, my blue Malibu slid and spun around facing in the other direction. I was terrified so I got out of the car. The police arrived and I asked them to call Tommy. One officer stood with me by the side of the road as we looked at my car. He said, "This is such a dangerous stretch of road; accidents happen here very often." As if on cue, a car slammed into my sitting Malibu.

Finally, Tommy arrived. But to my chagrin, instead of being happy I wasn't injured, he angrily yelled at me for wrecking 'his' car. Our car insurance dropped us. When I inquired as to why Allstate would not continue to insure us as the police report showed the accident was not my fault; I was shocked to hear the reasoning. "You were driving your car into oncoming traffic," he calmly told me. When I explained my car swerved that way and the police report indicated I was not at fault; he said I didn't send him the report so they went with what the other driver said. "You're in good hands with Allstate"- yeah, right.

Eventually, the last car Tommy ever bought me before our divorce was one I chose. When we visited the cheaper Saturn dealership, I noticed with excitement, the used Mustang on the lot. I had always admired the design of the Mustang since I was in high school. For my taste, a used Mustang was way better than any new Saturn. I happily became the new owner.

Tommy, my daughter Jill, and I lived in New Jersey. Wherever we went, he always drove with the top down. When Jill was eight months old, we moved to Iowa, where he still drove with the convertible top down. One time we were driving on the road, when suddenly the car (and our family, of course) was covered with a fine dust. The paved street had become a dirt path! I found it very funny; he was so mad.

Less than two years after we arrived in Iowa, we moved back to New Jersey. It was not until later, when Jill was near to completing high school, that I felt I could finally file for my long-awaited divorce. When I told Tommy, he got even more violent and crazy as he put a loaded gun to my cheek and threatened to shoot me. He then thought the better of it and beat me instead. Seeing my injuries, the police recommended I obtain a restraining order against him and then they escorted him to the mental ward of our local hospital. During that year of our separation, Tommy was released to live with his mother, but Jill would not go back to school for her senior year because her father had embarrassed her in front of her schoolmates. We found a solution: I lived in the marriage house, and Jill lived with a family (whose children she babysat) so she could finish her senior year at a new school. I gave her my Mustang to drive to her new school and I took a bus to work. She loved it and because of it, Jill became very popular with the kids at her new school.

Finally free of a hurtful marriage and living on my own, I chose a stylish, used, awesome black, and very powerful '89 Grand Am. Since it's the only car I ever bought by myself. This vehicle kept me safe as I followed the moving truck from New Jersey to Maryland where my sister lives.

Years after settling down in Leisure World, my daughter Jill gifted me her 2001 small, cute, gold Kia. It is the last car I will ever need since I'm within walking distance of everything I need now; and the Leisure World Shuttle can take me where I need to go when I can no longer drive.

Lastly, after my husband's purchase of a new and all totally electric powered Chevy Bolt, we now own the best looking, easiest to handle, quietest, smoothest, and by far the best car I've ever been in!

Reflections (Butterflies)

Once I was taking a walk on the golf course (near my house) on my
way from my home to Clubhouse I.

There was this gorgeous Monarch butterfly who seemed to join me on
my usually kinda long walk.

She kept me company and before I knew it - I was there!

Thank God for butterflies.

They do so much more than decorate our beautiful world.

And so Butterflies lived peacefully in our world with Mankind forever
after - (in a Perfect World, that is).

145

Childhood Menagerie

"If no one wants this kitten, I'm going to drown it." It was twilight eve when this alarming announcement came from a camper holding up a tiny, adorable, solid black kitty as he crossed in front of us to move on; going from tent to tent looking for someone to save her.

"We'll take it!" my ex and I cried out at once. I reached out and as soon as he put the sweet, innocent kitten into my outstretched hands, I tenderly hugged her to my chest. Our daughter Jill, only 8 months old, squealed with delight. "Let's call her Twilight," I declared as we got down on the ground to let joyful Baby Jill stroke and pet Twilight to her heart's content.

Jill was unable to pronounce our new kitty's name, so we called her "T." We gave Twilight (T) some water, milk, and bread. A box with something soft in it became Twilight's temporary bed. The next morning our family now including T, along with our neighbors with their two small kids, packed everything up into our car and headed back home.

As it happened, we arrived on the 4th of July. With precious little Jill safely sleeping in her crib and cute T asleep in her makeshift bed, my ex and I went to the roof of our house to enjoy the fireworks display. When the sky show ended, I went in to kiss Jill and pet T. To my dismay, Twilight was gone! So, even though it was late at night, this was urgent. During our long vacation, new neighbors along with two huge dogs, had moved in next door to us. With all the noise of the fireworks, we didn't hear the loud barking that must have frightened our tiny T into running for her life. Still, I went door-to-door praying someone had taken our scared little kitty in for safe keeping. But I walked home alone.

Baby Jill and I were brokenhearted. And my ex would not allow me to get another kitten. So, I bought Jill a pitch black kitten hand puppet, and named him "Midnight." From then on, I collected many puppets of different animals and characters (including a clown) to delight Jill. Then even before she was two, Jill put on puppet shows. During her two year old birthday month, we moved back from Iowa to our home state of New Jersey.

Teacher's Certificate in hand, I landed a job in a Day Care Center permitting me to bring toddler Jill along. As she grew older, my precocious Jill helped me care for the younger tots.

Jill was eight years old when we sent away for a pollywog. The pet for Jill arrived "Special Delivery" and included a container of water, food, and instructions. The two of us were mesmerized as we enjoyed observing the stages of the little tadpole's fascinating metamorphosis to frog. Jill named him "Froggy Woggles" and excitedly brought him to school for show and tell. She shared that she had watched this amazing pollywog develop into a very small green frog who lived totally underwater.

Years later, Froggy Woggles was vibrantly alive, growing bigger, and still always underwater. During a trip to the country, Jill noticed and ran after a tiny brown spotted frog that was hopping along. When she caught him, we brought him home. The second pet was smaller and even cuter than Froggy Woggles, but Jill loved them both with the same intensity. Her land frog eventually died. Good thing for Jill that Froggy Woggles was still with her.

Although Foggy Woggles lived entirely underwater, Jill now eleven years old, began creating cartoons featuring him and his friends. In the cartoons she created, Froggy Woggles not only lived on land; he also went to school and did all the things that Jill did. Those creative cartoon panels depicting entire stories or jokes, amused me and our Iowa neighbors when I sent the cartoon strips to them. With my help, Jill sent copies of her comic strips to many magazines. Mostly she heard back, "Thanks, but no thanks." Until the happy day when one not only liked her cartoon strip, they promised to publish it and as payment, they would send her a copy of the magazine it appears in. This was great news.

But there was also sad news. After living a long life, her beloved Froggy Woggles was sick and dying. Before the day was out, he had passed away. I tried to comfort Jill by saying he will live forever in her heart and her cartoons.

We went next to the pet store where Jill picked out the best, most beautiful blue parakeet, and sometime later, two friendly hamsters.

Although wishing for another kitten, Jill happily enjoyed playing with them, especially the fluffy one that Jill named "Puffball" because her light tan fur was so soft. We let Puffball out to wander on the grass because she loved to nibble clover before returning to her cage.

Also, Jill won two goldfish at our local fair. As Jill was growing up, we also gifted her with an amazing silver colored baby bunny, gerbils, plus an aquarium. Jill got to pick out the tropical fish for it. She chose clever names for each and every one of her pets including all of her fish.

Finally, in Jill's junior year of high school after her father and I separated, her long-time dream of being the mama to a black kitten came true. At the animal shelter, Jill fell in love with, adopted, and named her black kitten with bright yellow eyes, "Saffron Ambrosia." This is the pet she had been longing for since Twilight ran away from home when Jill was just a baby.

Jill is now a Mom to three children with two cats, a dog, and an aquarium filled with fish, their own Childhood Menagerie. The very first pet Jill got for her family was another little black kitten.

Springtime in Maryland

Cherry blossoms open on their trees

Daffodils bloom so yellow with green leaves
Among a bed of tiny purple violets

Around the bend a single daffodil almost seems
Lonely as it sways in the breeze

Birdsong fills the air; Spring is here!

Jill's Windy Wedding

It was a warm but windy day, one simply wonderful weekend in September. Jill had wished for a wedding on the sand by the ocean for as long as she could remember; and that day was soon to come. In fact, today was the very day!

All of us came, her friends and family, and even her puppy dog Solo was welcome, until he wasn't and he had to leave the soft sand.

We all sat happily on yoga mats waiting until their wedding began. My husband and I were there of course: the parents of the Bride. Our grandchildren, 12 and 14 too had on the sea green colors like those our niece Maid of Honor Laura and the Bridesmaids wore. Our little grandnephew Elliot, only four, looked so cute in his big bow tie and red floppy hat that tied under his chin. He was dig, dig, digging a hole so deep in the sand "for the bad guys to fall in."

Our granddaughter Avalon found a pebble shaped like a heart! And just then, wouldn't you know it; the wedding did start!

I watched in fascination, the futile preparation of the Wedding Arch that kept blowing down. In matching gowns, Laura and all the Bridesmaids and five Groomsmen put it up again, blew down; up again, blew down, this went on even now that the wedding has begun.

First came Avalon helping the little flower girl to spread red rose petals that floated our way, drifting on the breeze. Then the little ring bearer runs up to the front as happy as you please.

Our grandson Malachi walked his mom Jill, our beautiful Bride all dressed in white down the aisle. Yet the wind was so strong the planned music was gone, so the Bridesmaids all sang Da da da-da, Da da da-da and arriving at the right of the fallen arch with the ocean behind them, happy Jill and Sean were wed. They continued without a second thought when Jill's sheer lacy white bridal veil was whisked off by the wind (I watched as it then sailed away wildly on a windy breeze to the ocean that seemed to be waving its congratulations and in celebration of this marvelously warm wedding day.)

We all blew bunches of bubbles for the Bride and Groom, now husband and wife, who in this blended family with three kids between them (Avalon, Malachi, and Xavier) will live happily together for the rest of their lives.

♦ ♦ ♦ ♦ ♦

About the Author

Joanie was born into a family filled with art and music. She played piano and guitar at home; viola in her high school orchestra, and the Glockenspiel in the marching band.

Joanie won art scholarships to three colleges and finished with a BA in Fine Arts and Teacher's Certificate. In addition, she was trained as a medical records technician. She has won prizes for her artwork, had two one-woman shows, a small business creating pastel paintings of fruit, flowers, favorite toys, pets, and people.

In New Jersey, Joanie was a substitute teacher, Medical Records Technician, and then for about 10 years as the Secretary to the Vice President of a major bank. She also volunteered at the local library.

When she moved to Maryland, she volunteered at a Jewish Rehab until her clearance was approved for her job in the Justice Department in the Federal Government where she worked for 19 years until her retirement in 2017, when she was free to pursue her hobbies full time.

Writing stories and poems, sketching, reading, and painting are among her favorite things, along with taking long walks alone or with friends, singing with musical groups, and playing games or talking with friends. Combining friendship with writing, Joanie loves sharing her essays and poems with her new friends in the Writers Group of Leisure World.

CHAPTER 9

THOUGHTS, OBSERVATIONS, AND A STORY

By Steven P. Marini

A Man from Uncle

Perhaps we all have someone in our life whom we greatly admire among family and friends. The person's story may have begun before yours did, perhaps by a few years or a generation ahead. It is common for a child to look up to an older person in the family. There must be something in human nature to that.

Aside from instinct, there are bound to be elements of their story that are striking, specific actions, events or achievements that set the person apart. They build the pedestal for their perch. It takes time.

My uncle's story began with World War II. The shocking news of Pearl Harbor in 1941 lit a fire in many young American men, sending them off to enlist in the military. He chose the Marine Corps. He was only five-foot six, but showed a rugged presence with a strong, deep voice, and he was smart.

In a newspaper interview in 2018, he described some of the action he endured in the brutal six-month Battle of Guadalcanal. It included sleeping in a foxhole for 45 days. If it rained, you slept in water. There were continuous Japanese bombing raids. The enemy attacked an American airfield that the Marines defended from a perch up on a ridge. On the 45th day, he was wounded severely by mortar fire and was awarded the Purple Heart. There were field promotions. By the end of the war he was a Lieutenant.

As a civilian, he began living the "American Dream," marrying my mother's sister, getting a college education, and starting a family with three children. With a career in education, life was good.

But then the Korean War shook him from the dream. In 1950, the Marines called again, after all he had been through in WW II. He declined an offer from his school principal to "pull some strings" for him. He had to go. In a conversation with my cousin, I learned he was called back because he was a junior officer, a group of veterans sorely needed. So, he returned to battle as a company commander.

After three and a half years, he had to make a decision between taking a promotion to Major and staying in the Marines or going back into civilian life. He chose a career in public education. It was a good move.

All was well for a while until he faced another tragic challenge. Living in Massachusetts, his beautiful, funny, loving wife and mother of his kids, my Aunt Leona, died of breast cancer in 1957. He was a single father. It must have been an enormous struggle. He worked weekends with the Post Office to make ends meet, so sometimes my family took the kids on a Saturday and his sister did the same at other times.

However, Uncle Gene always found strength in moving on. He soon met a lovely widow with children a bit older than his own and they were married. But life wasn't through creating a rough path for Gene DeFelice, not by a long shot. In a few years, his second wife took ill and died. He was about forty.

In half a lifetime, Gene had been nearly killed in a war, taken away from his family by a second war, lost his first wife, and later a second wife to disease while raising three children. What would the second half of his life bring, happiness or more challenge? He had faced so much. What was to come?

His career went very well and eventually he became the principal of Canton Junior High School in Massachusetts. Fortunately for him, he met an attractive woman who was the girls Physical Education teacher. They married and enjoyed a long, happy life together. They settled on Martha's Vineyard.

But there was yet another major twist in his life story. One night while at home on Martha's Vineyard, there was a knock on his door. He opened it to see a young man, probably in his forties. The man asked, "Are you Gene DeFelice?"

"Yes," replied Gene.

"Well, I am your son."

Imagine getting a surprise that you have a new son. Apparently, he had a girlfriend before going off to war and, unbeknownst to Gene, they produced a baby boy. He had no knowledge of this, having had no contact with the former girlfriend. My cousin said that there was no doubt about the truth. One could tell by just looking at him who the man's father was. The new son was welcomed into the family.

My uncle, Eugene DeFelice, retired Captain, United States Marine Corps, and a former Principal of Canton Junior High, passed away recently at 98. If John F. Kennedy were alive today, he would have to add a chapter in his book, "Profiles in Courage," to my Uncle Gene.

A Way Out

Tonight could be a winner for Davey.

He'd been on a long losing streak at the track and couldn't afford much more. He was familiar with some of the horses running tonight, their strengths and their weaknesses. He felt good.

Davey Esteban was part Hispanic, part Afro-American, a twenty-eight-year-old living in Dedham, Massachusetts. He had not finished high school and barely got by as a pizza delivery man at Rocco's Pizza and Subs in Needham. He spent his off nights at the track trying to make his dream come true. It was a tough task. Mostly, he just made things worse.

The weather at the track was clear, had been for several days. Then why did he lose in the first three races? He could not understand it. He knew these horses. He should be winning.

The fourth race would be a different story. Davey hit a seven-to-one long shot, making back most of his losses. He celebrated with some beers and then put half his winnings in the sixth, spreading it out over three strong possibilities in the trifecta. His confidence was growing. A great feeling.

He picked third place, but one and two eluded him. The track had sucked away more of his hard earned cash. "Damned this track," he yelled at nobody. A couple more beers might help. He drank slowly.

Davey studied his racing form. He saw a horse he liked, a winner for him before. It could win again. But as he approached the betting window, the odds on his horse climbed to fifteen-to-one. Could be a nice payoff. But it didn't happen. Once again, his money went down a hole.

Davey was getting a strong buzz from the beer. He bought another. Holding the paper beer cup in his left hand, he thrust his right into his pants pocket, pulling out all the cash he had left. Not much. He didn't notice the large, tough looking man in the dark suit watching him.

"Hey, young fellow," said the suit. "Looks like you can't get a break tonight."

"What? Who are you?"

"Name's Sal DiFino. What's yours?"

"Davey Esteban. You been watching me or something?"

"Sort of. I play the horses, but I also play people. I watch and observe. I saw you win one earlier. You can do it again."

"Damned right I can." Davey looked at the few bucks left in his hand.

"I guess you're running a little short, kid. Maybe I can help you out."

"What? Why would you want to do that?"

"Like I said, I play people, too. I watch what kind of bets people make. It tells me if they know what they're doing or not. You've made some good choices tonight, but you just didn't get a break. Let me loan you some cash for the next race. Bet it any way you like. You'll be okay."

"Really?" said Davey. "You'll do that?"

Sal reached inside his coat pocket and pulled out some crisp cash. He handed a hundred dollars to Davey. "Go for it, Davey."

So, Davey went for it. He bet fifty on the number five horse to win and twenty on the number eight to place. Number five came through a winner, paying off at three-to-one, one hundred and fifty bucks for Davey. He whooped and hollered as if he'd just won a million.

Davey paid Sal DiFino his hundred bucks and pocketed the rest. It felt good.

"Thanks, Mr. DiFino. I really appreciate this."

"No trouble, Davey. And call me Sal. Look, I got to run. Why don't I meet you here tomorrow night and we can make some more money together?"

"Yeah. That'd be great, Mr.....er, Sal. I'll call in sick. See you tomorrow night."

The next night, Sal was there as promised. He bought Davey a beer and followed him up to the betting window. Davey studied his racing form as he walked. He was grinning.

"I feel good tonight, Sal. I know I'm going to get some winners."

"Yeah, me too, Davey." Sal did not smile. It was not his nature. He watched Davey as he placed his bet at the window, like a lion watches a wildebeest, the one trailing the herd.

The losses came heavy for Davey until he was broke. He could not believe he was losing. But Sal was there to help him out. He loaned Davey money, as much as Davey wanted. Sal said he knew Davey was good for it, so Davey kept sinking deeper into debt with Sal.

This went on for a few weeks. One night, Sal suggested that Davey come back to the track again, but Davey explained that he could only come to the track on his nights off. Davey told him about his job at Rocco's Pizza and Subs in Needham Center.

The next night, Sal called in sick for Davey. Another night of great expectations. It gave Davey a high. But it was another night of betting and losing. Davey and Sal agreed to try again next week.

But Sal had other business in mind. They met in the parking lot, about thirty minutes before most people arrived. Sal eased his large, powerful body into the passenger seat of Davey's car and explained how the game would now be played. Sal told Davey that he had good news and bad news. The good news was that he was going to give Davey a chance to pay back his debt by performing certain odd jobs. The bad news was that those jobs were illegal enterprises. Sal laughed as if he had made a joke.

Davey had no choice but to play ball with Sal. He was doing Sal's dirty work all around Boston; collecting extortion money, threatening store owners, and even roughing up a drug addict prostitute who Sal thought was trying to cheat him. This game was getting scary.

After a couple of weeks, Davey decided he couldn't do it anymore and informed Sal that he had enough. But Sal doesn't take no for an answer. He hit Davey hard in the gut, again and again. Davey buckled over in pain. As he straightened up, Sal slapped him across the face, drawing blood from Davey's mouth. A chill ran down his spine and his mouth went dry.

"Don't forget, Davey boy that you're in this up to your ears now. You've extorted people, delivered drugs, collected from prostitutes. You could spend many years in prison. Better be a good boy or what you got tonight will just be a mosquito bite compared to what you'll get next."

Davey continued to do Sal's bidding. Sal would show up at Rocco's pizza shop when he had a job for Davey, order a pizza and slip a note to Davey with instructions about his next job. Davey wondered how long this could go on. Would Sal reach a point where he didn't need Davey anymore? Then what? He never expected this. He wanted to find a way out.

Davey had seen television shows where a mobster would snitch to the FBI about bad guys and the Bureau would protect him, in fact, put him in hiding with a whole new identity. Davey had no family so maybe that would work for him. He called the Boston office of the FBI.

The call was taken by Special Agent Robert Nelson, a man with a lot of experience dealing with the Mob. He asked Davey to come in and tell him the whole story. Davey agreed.

"Thanks Mr. Nelson. I'm real glad you're going to help me. I've got to get out of this mess. I'm afraid Mr. Difino's going to kill me when he doesn't need me anymore."

"Relax, Davey," said Agent Nelson. "We're not going to let that happen to you."

"Thanks. When can you get me away from here?"

"Well, Davey, it doesn't work exactly like that. First, we need your help to prove that DiFino is responsible for these crimes. You need to help us gather solid evidence."

"You mean I've got to testify against him? Won't that be kind of dangerous?"

"No, no, Davey. We can't arrest him until we observe him committing a crime or we collect significant evidence against him regarding a crime. So, to start, we need you to tell the whole story again, this time to a stenographer who'll type it up into what's called a deposition. Then you look it over, make sure we've got it right, and then you sign it. That's the first step. Then you go home and go about your normal business. That's very important for you."

"Will I be safe?"

"Absolutely."

"Should I go to work tonight?"

"Yes, Davey. Act normal. We'll put an agent inside the pizza shop undercover."

Davey left the building cautiously and drove home. He had several hours before work.

Agent Nelson called Special Agent Tammy Watson into his office after Davey left. The FBI knew DiFino worked for Tommy Shea, a Mob kingpin from Somerville. Agent Watson had worked undercover for years trying to pry information from him. Agent Nelson wanted the big fish.

The FBI made arrangements to have Tammy Watson work the same shift as Davey Esteban, although Rocco was a bit nervous about the whole thing. Nonetheless, he complied.

The FBI didn't know they had a problem with Tammy Watson. For eighteen months, she not only worked undercover with DiFino. She worked under the covers with him, too. She grew quite attracted to the strong tough guy and had sold out to him. She gave the FBI bits of nearly worthless information about DiFino and Shea's enterprises. DiFino gave Tammy a lot more.

Davey reported to work as usual and was introduced to the new employee working behind the counter. He was surprised at first but realized she might be the FBI plant. He couldn't ask her, though, so he just eyed her. She returned his stare with a blank look.

Davey made several deliveries early and then there was the usual rush of orders during the five to seven o'clock period. Just after ten, an order came in for a mushroom and sausage pizza with an address at the outskirts of town near the Charles River. He put the pizza in a warming bag and placed it on the floor in the front of his car. He looked all around before getting in.

He headed out on Dedham Avenue and turned left at South Street. It was a dark, heavily wooded neighborhood. He found the address and pulled into the end of a long driveway, leaving the engine run as he took the pizza to the front door. All was calm in this wooded part of town.

Davey rang the bell and waited. Soon, a short, heavy-set man answered the door. "Yes," he said. "Can I help you?"

"I'm just delivering your pizza, Mister."

"I didn't order a pizza. Hey, Hun, did you order a pizza?"

A voice came from another room. "Nope, not me."

"You sure you got the right address, kid?" said the man.

"Yeah, got it right here." He showed the order ticket to the man.

"Well, that's my address, but we didn't order any pizza."

"Gee, I'm sorry, Mister, but this is the address I got."

"No problem, kid. Say, what kind of pizza is it?"

"Mushroom and sausage."

"You know what, I'll take it."

"Well, OK. I don't want to take it back anyway. Thanks, Mister."

The man paid for the pizza and Davey walked back to his car. He had turned the headlights off, so it was dark near his car. He was happy the man took the pizza, and, for the moment, it took his mind off his current troubles. He didn't think about Sal DiFino and his Mob business. He didn't think about the FBI and how they were going to help him. Most of all, he didn't think there would be someone hiding in the back of his car on the floor with a knife.

Davey desperately wanted out of his trouble with Sal DiFino. The FBI offered him a way out. He never knew the Bureau unknowingly, through a connection to DiFino with a dirty agent named Tammy Watson, had set up another way out for him. As a hired punk with a knife slashed his throat, Davey found a way out.

This Competition is Criminal

Scribes love to write about competitors, especially in sports. Pitchers versus pitchers (Koufax vs Clemens); hitters versus hitters (Williams vs DiMaggio); center fielders (Mays vs Mantle); quarterbacks (Brady vs Manning); basketball (Russell vs Chamberlain); and tennis (Borg vs McEnroe).

But there is competition in other fields. Concert pianists compete. Actors and musicians compete for shiny Oscar and Grammy awards. Scientists compete for the Noble Prize. Journalists compete for the Pulitzer Prize. But here's an occupation that you never hear about as being competitive: Crime.

Therefore, I propose a competition for, "Outstanding Performance by an Individual in a High Stakes Robbery." No supporting players in this contest, so no gangs are in the running.

Here are my nominees, in chronological order based on the year of the heist:

1 - Thomas Randele, Cleveland, Ohio 1969

2 - D.B. Cooper, Portland, Oregon 1971

Here are their stories:

#1: Randele's real name was Ted Conrad who was a young teller at a bank in Cleveland, Ohio. On July 11, 1969, after his 20th birthday, he finished his shift and walked out with a large paper bag containing $215,000 (more than $1.6 million today) and was never seen again. When he failed to show up for work on Monday morning, the bank manager realized the money was missing. Ted Conrad and the money stayed missing for fifty-two years. That is a very, very long period of deception. He sure could keep a secret.

According to investigators, Thomas Randele, was a very good man, a good father, a good husband, a good friend, and a pro golfer - he seemed to be well-liked by everybody. Numerous acquaintances have come forward to attest to his good nature and pleasant personality. He lived the perfect life of a fugitive on the run.

The key to his success was that Conrad took on a new identity and a new life, staying a jump head of law enforcement for fifty-two years. The case was even featured on television shows including "America's Most Wanted" and "Unsolved Mysteries," but he remained elusive. His success continued until his death in May 2021. He was seventy years old, close to a normal full life, when he died of cancer.

He had been the assistant golf pro at the Pembroke Country Club in Massachusetts, playing on the professional winter tour in Florida in the offseason and became the full-time manager of the country club. Eventually, he began a successful career in luxury automotive sales for close to 40 years. He also became an excellent self-taught cook. He and his family lived in a small, three-bedroom house.

Cold-case investigators discovered multiple connections between Thomas Randele and Ted Conrad from his newspaper death notice. For example, both attended New England College in New Hampshire. Several documents signed by both Randele and Conrad had matching handwriting.

Thomas Randele made a deathbed confession to his family, telling them who he really was. He is survived by his wife, Kathy, and his daughter, Ashley. Their lives have been changed forever.

#2: On November 24, 1971, a plain looking man in a business suit calling himself Dan Cooper, purchased a one-way ticket to Seattle, Washington. His story has become an American legend. Shortly after 3:00 p.m., he gave the stewardess a note saying that he had a bomb in his briefcase. In a way, he did.

Cooper opened the case, showing the stewardess a quick look at a mass of wires and red colored sticks, resembling dynamite. He told her to inform the Captain, which she did. She told the Captain that he wanted four parachutes and $200,000 in cash. Today that seems like a trifle amount for all the effort.

When the plane landed in Seattle, Cooper got what he wanted in exchange for the flight's 36 passengers. Cooper kept the flight crew members, and the plane took off heading for Mexico City. Hours later Cooper did something hard to believe. He jumped out of the back of the plane with the money. Although the plane landed safely in Mexico City, Cooper was gone into the night sky. Many think Cooper could not have survived the jump. The parachute could not be steered and he was dressed in clothes not suited for such a jump. He was not a veteran jumper. Some of the money was found in 1980, about five thousand dollars. The serial numbers matched the cash that Cooper was given, but the case has never been closed.

So, who is the GOAT (Greatest Of All Time) among the big money thieves? If success is the determining factor, I know who I vote for. Do you?

The Greatest Thrill in Sports

Ted Williams, the Hall of Fame baseball player, used to claim that the hardest thing to do in sports is to hit a baseball. Using a round bat to hit a round ball squarely was the toughest thing to do successfully in all of sports. That may be, but I'm thinking about what gives a player the greatest thrill, something so satisfying that the memory will last a lifetime Here's a clue. It is related to Ted's thinking. Here is mine.

Let's think for a while about what some great athletic thrills may be. How about scoring a touchdown in football? I had that experience in the ninth grade. It was truly awesome.

We had started interscholastic football for the first-time when I was fourteen years old. I was the starting fullback. We had a pass play where the ends went deep and I crept up to the line of scrimmage, pretended to block for a second or two and then went down field about five yards and cut to the right. The quarterback zoomed the ball to me. I took it in a steady run and immediately turned downfield with the sideline near me on my right. (Heisman Trophy winner, Joe Bellino, called the outside, meaning near the sideline, a runner's best friend). I looked up and saw no defenders in front of me. I turned on the gas and raced to the endzone, scoring our team's first Touchdown of the year. It was thrilling, but was it the greatest thrill one could have? Nah.

I cannot imagine scoring a goal in sports like ice hockey, soccer, or field hockey are among the greatest thrills, although they must be good. I scored a couple of goals in college lacrosse and that was nice, but not the greatest.

I never played competitive tennis, but I cannot see anything there that might qualify. Winning a tournament, a match, or even a set can take a very long time and I'm talking about something that happens in an instant that lifts you up in an emotional high. You get to bask in the glory of the moment.

There is a "hole in one" in golf, but the only experience I have with that is from a pitch and putt game. There is some skill involved, but there is also a lot of luck. Buona fortuna (Italian for 'Good Luck'). So, what is the greatest thrill in sports? I'll describe it based on my own experience. It happened in the spring of 1960. It was a Pony League baseball game, the 13 and 14 age group. My team, the Wildcats, were taking on the Panthers.

When I came to bat, the bases were empty. I don't remember the count or the pitcher. But I remember the left fielder. His name was

Paul Newman. No, not that one. This one didn't resemble a movie star who was so good looking and cool that even the guys wanted to be like him. This one had short cut hair and a chubby round build like a milk bottle. He didn't look like he could catch a basketball thrown his way.

The pitch came in rather slowly. It had to because I would never have pulled it to left otherwise. I did not possess what is referred to as a quick bat. But I did have a smooth swing. I let it rip. History being made.

The contact was a solid, sharp pop sound. It was better than a "crack of the bat." There was not even the slightest rattle in the bat, almost as if I hadn't hit it at all. It felt perfect. It was "good wood."

As I ran up the baseline, I knew I had something. The unbelievable happening right before me. I remember the sound of my manager, Buck, yelling at the ball, "Get out. Get out." It did.

I briefly watched poor Paul. He saw the ball in flight, it was coming his way and soaring over him. The toughest fly ball to catch is one going right over your head. Poor Paul tried to turn to his left, but his feet seemed tied together. All he could do was watch as the ball left the field. It disappeared into the trees.

I had experienced the greatest thrill in all of sports. I was lost in my personal Twilight Zone.

"You are about to enter another dimension, a dimension not only of sight and sound but of mind. A journey into a wondrous land of imagination."

I was circling the bases, lost in my world of euphoria. I felt like I should shout out the words Cagney screams at the end of his great film, White Heat. "Top of the world, MA! Top of the world!"

I slowed from a run to a trot. I heard my teammates yell and cheer for me, but I couldn't see them. They were in real time, and I was still in the Zone.

Second base. The tip of the diamond. I touched the edge of the bag and moved on. Third base, the hot corner. My opponents on their bench were silent, like their dogs had all died.

I headed for home. The sound of my teammate's cheers grew loud again as I got closer to the plate. I stepped on it quickly in stride and headed for the bench. They were all standing, patting me on the back and shaking my hand as I passed by. I accepted their adulation with princely dignity. There was no dancing or trash talking back then. We were way too cool for that. There is no trash talking in the Twilight Zone.

So, there you have it. The greatest thrill in sports is - - hitting a homerun OVER a fence. No inside the park stuff. The ball must go over a fence. Elvis must leave the building. Did you hear that, Ted Williams? I conquered the unconquerable.

◆ ◆ ◆ ◆ ◆

About the Author

Steven P. Marini holds a Master's degree in Educational Technology from Boston University and a B.A. in Business Administration from New England College. He has spent over thirty years in the Education and Training, including positions in higher education and the federal government. Although he describes himself as a "card carrying New Englander," he lived for twenty-six years in Maryland while pursuing a career as a project manager spanning four federal agencies. A "Baby Boomer," Steve started fiction writing as he moved into retirement on Cape Cod. He has published five murder mysteries while on the Cape, but this changed in 2017 as more grandkids appeared in the family in Maryland. So, it was time to move back. He and his wife, Louise, now live in Silver Spring, Maryland and he has resumed writing, moving into the world of Erotic Romance.

CHAPTER 10

PASSING BY

By Bobbie Troy

Study in Blue and Green

She remembered seeing a painting, A Study in Blue and Green, in one of the prison art books. (Yes, they have a great library). It was an abstract in blue and green, reminding her of lush acres of grass on her grandfather's farm and endless blue skies, a time when they would picnic as a family.

But something went suddenly wrong the night she met Nick in the local bar. She did not know that a friend of a friend had a gun, and when she ran from the scene, that was her first mistake.

Now, three years later, she was still poring over A Study in Blue and Green, knowing that she had another three years of Gray and Black.

Dead Man's Mountain

That morning, we agreed to meet about 5:00 p.m. at the foot of Dead Man's Mountain. It was really only a sand dune, but the highest one on the beach. And at that time of night, the sun would almost be one with the sea, creating a special ambiance. The romance was palpable. I couldn't wait.

This was the first evening that Paul and I would be alone. His family, like mine, vacationed at this beach every year since I could remember. We were childhood friends. But it was different now that we were both thirteen.

We were unsure what we were supposed to do and feel. Suddenly, a whole new world was opening up for us, and we wanted to find our way ahead. I knew that we were on the same page; words were not necessary.

The temperature had dropped a bit, so I hugged myself to keep warm while waiting for Paul. Then his lanky silhouette appeared not far from me. We didn't say a word. He just took my hand and we started walking up the dune.

The Old Age Repository [1]

Wake up, Grandma. We're here.

Huh, huh? Oh, ya mean the old age repository?

Grandma, please. It will be ok. You'll see. Look how pretty is it up there on the hill.

I still can't believe yur doin' this ta me, Sonny. I practically raised ya up. Now yur dumpin' me off like so much garbage. That's all I am ta ya? OK, OK. Have it yur way. Get on home now. At least ya've still got a home ta go ta.

Granny, we went all over this. Look at your leg. It's broken in five places. If I hadn't stopped by your place after work, you'd be dead by now. I just couldn't leave you alone anymore.

Yeah, well. Maybe dead is better than dumped.

****

---

[1] Originally published 6/20/11:
https://cavalcadeofstars.wordpress.com/2011/06/20/bobbie-troy/

Hi, Mr. Johnson. Before you go up to see your Grandmother, I would like to talk to you. Please come into my office.

Thank you, Doctor. What is it? Is Grandma OK? Does she like it here? She can be stubborn if she sets her mind against something.

Well, she's OK. Physically, that is. But mentally she's having a hard time adjusting. She's aloof, and well, I'm afraid she's retreated into another reality. That's fairly common with newcomers to our facility. But she should get over it in time and adjust perfectly fine. So for now, just go along with whatever she says.

Yes, Doctor, I guess you know best. But I really don't know what you're talking about.

****

Hi, Grandma. Your room looks nice with all your pictures out. I brought you some candy. Grandma, aren't you going to say hi?

Why should I? I'm busy. We're outta control. Spinnin' outta orbit. I'm tryin' ta reach mission control to redirect our flight path, but nobody answers. So I have ta keep tryin'. Mission control, mission control, this is Granny123. Do ya read me? Do ya read me? I repeat, this is Granny123. Come in, mission control.

Look, just leave the candy, Sonny. I don't have time fur ya right now.

But Grandma, I came to visit all the way from the city. You know how long that takes. I want to make sure you're happy here. How's the food? Have you made any friends?

Mission control, mission control. Do ya read me? This is Granny 123. I repeat, this is Granny123. Come in, mission control.

Grandma, stop this nonsense. This isn't a spaceship. It's the Hillview Old Age Home. You know that. Now stop being silly. You know I love you, but I had no choice.

I don't know nuthin' but this is an old age repository that's outta orbit an' outta control. Just flingin' out space garbage every day. One comes in, one goes out. Garbage in, space garbage out. Nothin' more, Sonny. But when I get control, I'm gonna aim this baby at all the houses of all the relatives that dumped their loved ones in this old age repository. A smart meteor. That's what it 'ill be. A smart meteor that self-destructs after it's done the job. Then none of us 'ill have nuthin' to worry about.

****

Mission control, mission control, this is Granny123. Do ya read me?

Love Comes to Us [2]
(A wedding gift)

love comes to us
in many forms

like a soothing summer breeze
with its warmth and calm

like a surge within
that captures your heart before you know it
and everything in between

embrace the romance and the rapture
so they will always supersede routine

make each day totally yours to share
and carry through your private eternity

hold each other every day and every night
as if the world would stop without that touch

for love, above all else, with its magic and its mystery
will make you complete

---

[2] Originally published November 22, 2020:
https://cavalcadeofstars.wordpress.com/2020/11/22/bobbie-troy-32/

War Hero

a man stood on the sidewalk
with bloodshot eyes
like someone fired
a miniature shotgun
into both eye sockets

his fine merino wool coat
now full of holes
was a reminder of better days
of money, of happiness, and love

his right hand sporadically
grabbed at the surrounding air
as if trying to retrieve something
that was lost forever

his left hand was in the coat pocket
gently caressing a wooden box
with a Purple Heart
from the Vietnam War

his mouth could not speak
about the fear, the heat, the loss,
or the loneliness of battle
that made up the days

and his mind wondered how
he ended up on this sidewalk
alone

Can We Die From This?

can we die
from too much passion
unfilled dreams
lack of perspective

can we die from
the weight of reality
unknown love
the loss of hope

can we die from
lack of commitment
too much pain
disappointment

can we die from
unrealized goals
lack of desire
guilt and regret

can we die from
loneliness
too much anger
fear of dying

surely we can't
can we?

Of a Certain Age

I am of a certain age
where friends and family
are dying around me
faster than I can comprehend

this life is like
a trick of the light
one minute it's here
and the next it's gone

so I pick up my pen
and bemoan my fate
that I am still here
and it's getting late

Do Not Resuscitate

just another form
the doctors said
Do Not Resuscitate
that's in case ......

I know what it is
I said
If I sign this form
I will be, literally,
taking his breath away

Loneliness

now that he is gone
loneliness sits on my shoulders
in a torturous way

sometimes it's as quiet
as a baby's whimper
sometimes as loud
as machine gun fire

but if I wish it away
what will be my company
then?

Beyond Tomorrow [3]

if I could see
beyond tomorrow
I would collect
my laughter
in a jar
and save it
for the dark days
(you know the ones)

---

[3] Originally published 5/10/16: http://voxpoetica.com/tomorrow-2/

The Past

we wear the past
around our shoulders
like a cloak
that might protect us
from the future

we know the past
and savor it
plucking the good memories
and holding them close
while trying to push away
the bad, the difficult, and the sad

but the past
is all rolled into one
and is comforting
because we know it

Neuropathy Pain

my feet are burning
constantly
it feels like
someone sprayed them
with tiny, hot pellets
then walked away
and dared me
to live another day

Insomnia

insomnia lurks in the closet
and pounces on me
as I enter the bedroom

no, you don't, it says
I shall not serve you sleep
tonight or any night
and I wonder
what I did
to deserve this punishment

One Moment

perhaps a few seconds
maybe less
but not more
can spin us around
like a bullet
meant to do so

one moment
between love and hate
life and death
a moment
that can save or hurt
but only in hindsight

Circles and Hands [4]

If you hold your hands
behind your back
and walk in a circle three times
it will help you remember
what has eluded you
or so they say

If you hold your hands
in front of you
and walk in a circle three times
it will help you forget
your sorrows and woes
or so they say

if it were that simple
I would be circling every day
to remember the good things
and forget the bad

but the hands become old
and the circles get broken
and time passes on
or so they say

---

[4] Originally published 2012 in *Words Across Time*, by Windmore Foundation
for the Arts, Culpeper, VA.

Things I Should Have Said [5]

I should have said
that your tears
were like antique pearls
gracing porcelain cheeks

I should have said
that I would take those pearl tears
and turn them into happiness
if you gave me a chance

I should have said those things
but it was too late
your train had already left

Memories

memories are to be digested
slowly
like hors d'oeuvres
at a wedding feast
a bite of sweet
a bite of savory
chew, swallow, enjoy

---

[5] Originally published 4/27/2010:
http://poemblog.voxpoetica.com/2010/04/27/things-i-should-have-said.aspx

We Need to Believe [6]

we need to believe
in something
that we cannot touch
or feel emotionally
something within
or without
that is beyond seeing
beyond doubt
because sometimes
what we have
just isn't enough

She: In Desperation

she gulped her food down
quickly
as if trying to swallow
a piece of life
before it slipped away
and she would not have enough
to keep her going
for another day

---

[6] Originally published 3/26/18:
https://cavalcadeofstars.wordpress.com/2018/03/26/bobbit-troy-20/

When the Poetry Has Gone [7]

I feel empty sometimes
as if purpose and meaning
cannot be found
and I am afraid of today and tomorrow

I feel empty sometimes
even though my life has been full
and I've had more good times than bad

I feel empty sometimes
because passion and romance
now elude me
and even memories are fading

I feel empty sometimes
because the poetry has gone
and I don't know how
to get it back

Answers [8]

there are no answers
only people who think
they have answers

---

[7] Originally published 3/13/2019:
https://cavalcadeofstars.wordpress.com/2019/03/13/bobbie-troy-returns-5/
[8] Originally published 8/24/12: http://voxpoetica.com/two-by-bobbie-troy/

The Quiet

since he's been gone
the quiet
comes suddenly
like a March wind
and doesn't leave
until it's ready

the empty chair
the empty bed
speak loudly
to me

I shrug my shoulders
and know
that only time
might help me
live alone

Be Thankful

be thankful
to be "with"
and not "without"

it does not require
an idol, a god, a shout

but only the peace
that comes from the heart

when you are lucky
to be "with"
and not "without"

179

Bicycles and Butterflies

a friend
recently reminded me
that I used to be
an optimist

yes, I remember
those days
of my youth

when getting out of bed
was easy, not painful
and the day was a snap
whatever I chose to do

now I ponder
my predicament
it's called "aging"
and really don't see myself
as one of those "seniors"

who have
more nonlucid moments
than lucid
and spend their days
on a bench or doing puzzles

it was the job of youth

to keep us going

but we have been betrayed

by our bodies

yet, my friend reminds me

that I used to be

an optimist

and I must look

for that "self"

because she still exits

think of bicycles and butterflies,

she says

bicycles and butterflies

bicycles and butterflies

Faceless Women of the World [9]

we are your mothers, grandmothers, sisters, daughters

we are your wives, mistresses, and slaves

we have been revered and feared

by friends and family

often at the same time

we are your backbone, comfort, and peace

we are your adventure, shelter, and soul

---

9 Originally published 7/24/17:
https://cavalcadeofstars.wordpress.com/2017/07/24/bobbie-troy-16/

we have been loved and hated

by friends and family

often at the same time

we are a force, a wonder, an enigma

we are open, free, and fearless

we are ignored and loved

by friends and family

often at the same time

we are hope, love, and happiness

we are brightness, spirit, and optimism

we are cherished and forsaken

by friends and family

often at the same time

we are the sun, stars, and planets

we are morning, noon, and night

we are seen and unseen

by friends and family

often at the same time

we are the faceless women of the world

marching on through time

forging our destinies and yours

as we go on

and on

and on

I Speak to You [10]

I speak to you
not from the grave
but from the air
around you
the sun above
and the ground under your feet

I speak to you
as one who cherished
your love and friendship
shared with you joy and pain
and moved through life
feeling better
for knowing each other

I speak to you
not as a subscriber
to any belief of an afterlife
but to good memories
of all we were to each other
and all we were meant to be

I speak to you
as family and friend
and wish
that we may share
another moment together
somewhere between
being and nothingness

---

[10] Originally published 6/4/18:
https//cavalcadeofstars.wordpress.com/2018/06/04/bobbie-troy-22/

Passing By

when will we learn
that our footprint on this earth
means nothing
and everything
at the same time?

♦ ♦ ♦ ♦ ♦

About the Author

Bobbie Troy maintains her sanity and perspective on life by writing poetry, flash fiction, and original fairy tales with a 21st century twist. Within the Writers Group of Leisure World, she is known for her poetry. Her work is published widely online and in some print anthologies. Her poem, "Dear Diane," was nominated for a 2010 Pushcart Prize; her fairy-tale play, *Sasha and the Tree of Sorrows*, was produced in March 2011; and her poem, "Dear Diane (Letter 2)," was nominated for the 2012 Best of the Net. Bobbie also served on the Editorial Board for three anthologies. As a latecomer to the published author scene, Bobbie is proud of the fact that her first poem was published at the age of 62.

After retiring from a career in technical editing, Bobbie moved to Leisure World with her husband Sol in 2014. The Writers Group of Leisure World is a pivotal group in Bobbie's life in the community. The group provides intellectual stimulation, the opportunity to share creative writing with friends, and socializing after the meetings.

CHAPTER 11

LIFETIME OF LEARNING

By Woody Shields

To Tell the Truth

A television show from the 1950s, *To Tell the Truth*, featured three contestants with one central character sworn to be truthful and two imposters permitted to lie. Such deception during the early days of television exposed the American public to a world of fantasy. Similar to the television shows for adults, the make-believe Saturday morning cartoons conditioned children to accept talking animals with human characteristics. Seventy years later, our society continues to struggle with honesty and whom do we trust in a world of disinformation.

We are a nation of laws defined by a criminal code covering nearly every conceivable aspect of life. A code of conduct, defined as ethics, supplements the laws and provides acceptable standards for behavior. Regrettably in a direct challenge to ethical standards, our society also appears to establish standards for lying under certain circumstances and granted waivers for privileged professions.

The tolerance for lying in our society was (and remains) difficult to rationalize. In our personal relationships, we are permitted to lie to a person to avoid hurting a friend. However, all lies are not equal. The failure to honestly respond to the request for confirmation, such as "How do I look?" is quite different from cheating on a spouse.

In regard to different standards for lying, creditable surveys exist for a number of professions. To soften perceptions, the statisticians define the "most and least trusted professions." For several decades, nurses top the list as the "most trusted profession" followed closely by medical doctors, teachers, and military officers. A list of "least trusted professions" always includes politicians, lawyers, and car salesmen.

With regard to military officers, the professional standards require total honesty. The military cannot tolerate anyone that lies, cheats, or steals. Minor mistakes are allowed requiring temporary removal from the assignment and recertification. However, the failure to truthfully disclose a mistake is a loss of integrity and one's integrity can never be recertified.

On the other hand, total honesty for military leaders requires some discretion. Any information sworn to secrecy cannot be disclosed and must be protected for a lifetime. To compete with our adversaries, the military career of "Psychological Operations" was created where lying is officially sanctioned to confuse, deceive, and defeat our enemies. We can neither confirm nor deny.

The nature of lying complicates the conflict between the truth and the false. There are shades of lying such that the color of the lie may depend on whether or not the liar actually knows the lie is false. As an old proverb proclaims, "Be quick not to assume malice in matters of incompetence." Owing to the failures of our education system, we are frequently challenged with the unpleasant choice between malice and incompetence.

On the lowest rung of lying is a career in politics. Although politics may be a noble vocation, politics is always listed at the bottom of the "most trusted professions." The critics allude to the deceit in political debate when only the anticipated benefits of a position are cited while avoiding disclosure of the associated costs. The average politician is adept at avoiding the problem by answering a different question. The most successful politicians are blessed (or cursed) with an ease for lying. Similar to Saturday morning cartoons, humans can be trained to accept things that are not. Still, there is always considerable angst in the media when one politician accuses another of dishonesty. Both the pot and the kettle are equally tarnished.

Politics aside, we need to candidly evaluate our beloved hobby of writing. There are dozens of careers in writing. Many are based on a foundation of lying; that is, when the writer makes up a story (such as a novelist) or ghost writes any product for another (such as a speech writer). However, there exists respected writing careers (not based on lying) such as a news reporter, biographer, columnist, poet, lyricist, and technical writer.

A warning sign for the truthfulness of a writing product is the use of a pseudonym, a pen name. Although valid reasons may exist to use a pseudonym, such as privacy, the reluctance to sign one's name on the product is a notable clue to the factual content.

Understandably, the statisticians do not include various careers in writing in the survey of trusted professions. Several writing careers would likely fall below the politicians at the bottom of the list. Some writers have hit rock bottom and are digging deeper.

One of my writing mentors, an accomplished author of romance, described her occupation as "lying for a living" - an apparent waiver of responsibility. As fiction dominates the market, most book authors can be called liars - to include the renowned novelists. Whether they spin a tale to create suspense or to venture into the absurd, can the novelist ever be trusted? However, many would argue the insertion of creativity enriches a society.

The world of writing should be rather simple. A story or book can be either fiction or nonfiction. Nonetheless, the academics attempt to blur the lines between the right and the wrong with college courses in "Historical Fiction" and "Creative Nonfiction." How can we recognize the truth from the lies?

Sadly, the creative writers with their lies have infected other noble professions such as the theater, movies, and documentaries - creating a world of pretend. Actors may become famous for pretending to be someone they are not. The most amusing connection with politics is the absurdity of an actor (a professional liar) endorsing a politician (another professional liar). As expected, a number of actors become successful as politicians.

The world of advertising is similarly infested with lies and liars. The compensated spokesperson (normally an athlete or other famous person) will promote a product with their personal endorsement. The owner of the product, the sponsor, pays the spokesperson to read a prepared script. The spokesperson may never have used the product before the sponsor paid them to endorse the product. Nevertheless, the famous athlete swears total trust in the product. An endorsement is even less credible if the spokesperson is an actor (a professional liar). How many times have you seen a semi-retired actor espouse the benefits of a reverse mortgage that he has never used?

Likewise, a wildlife film producer admits many wildlife scenes are staged with rented animals, simulated habitat, superimposed sound effects, and creative lights. The storylines are written before filming. The reasoning is the ends justify the means. Wildlife documentaries are credited with raising awareness to protect the environment and threatened species.

The world of lying appears to have exploded during our lifetime. Amazon reports over one million new books are published each year; over ninety percent are fiction. In a hundred years, historians may gasp in amazement and wonder, "What were those people thinking?" and "How did we descend from such troubled minds?"

The only sin in writing is the fatal crime of stealing (plagiarism). Liars stealing from liars. Liars are protective of their lies and register their lies with the U.S. Copyright Office.

Given the dilemma of my career as a military officer (among the most trusted professions) in conflict with my aspiring writing career (among the least trusted professions), how do I proceed? What are the current rules for lying in our society and how do we recognize the difference? Who should we trust? Fortunately throughout my life, I have acquired a few survival tools to deal with our society of liars. Trust but a few. Always second check critical information. And most important, enjoy the show.

When They Were Young

The story is set several years ago when my son, William, was six and my daughter, Leslie, was four. Little sister Leslie would often drive William to the brink of frustration. As Leslie was brilliant she would stand behind William looking over his shoulder when he was doing math homework, do the math in her head, and announce the answer before he could finish the problem. Likewise, she would find his other homework assignments and write the answers for William to later discover.

After numerous requests for Leslie to stay away, one day William had enough and yelled, "You little bitch!" After separating the siblings and to establish the ground rules to avoid future conflicts, I took the opportunity (a teachable moment) to explain to William that a bitch is a female dog, and his sister is not a dog.

A few weeks later at my parent's home, Dad and I were sitting in the living room. William and his grandmother (my mother) were in the kitchen with our small female dog, a Pomeranian. We overheard William recounting his numerous difficulties with his sister and then he explained to my mother the difference between our dog, his sister, and a bitch. Dad and I listened quietly to the prolonged discussion as my mother attempted to understand the total context of William's frustration with his sister. A few minutes later, my red-faced mother entered the living room, sat down, and did not say a word.

Not to be outdone, William obtained revenge on his sister when he told the neighbor children that his parents were so mad at his sister they had her name changed to "Ugly." For the next several weeks, the neighbor boys asked, "Where's Ugly?"

Trust in Science

Science is the continuous process of discovery pushing the frontiers of the unknown. Our trust in science is at the foundation of scientific research. The success of our civilization may depend upon the proper application of science (present and future). How do we know when to trust the science and the experts who claim they are scientists?

Back to basics - in our youth we were taught the eight steps in the scientific method: observe, ask a question, gather information, form a hypothesis, test hypothesis, make conclusions, report, and evaluate.

Throughout our lives, we knowingly (or sometimes not) have used the scientific method. Learning from mistakes is a rite of passage into adulthood. As we mature, we understand the importance of faithfully completing each step of the scientific method. Miss one step, disaster may await. Although luck could intervene, consistent success requires compliance.

Beware, one can always find documentation to support any theory or conspiracy. Miracle products for pain relief and aliens on the moon compete with reports of progress in medical advances. The validity of the documentation requires the consumer to "Verify then Trust."

Every day we confront a variety of finite decisions that may have lifetime consequences, some are more important than others. As one example, we accept the science of air travel trusting our aircraft will depart the bounds of gravity and then safely return. Other decisions are not as easy to evaluate and require a complex assessment of risk, a probability (more likely than not) versus a near certainty.

We seem obsessed with the need to respond to a bad outcome to prevent any future occurrences. More often than not, we set the bar of expectation to perfection. However, determining the root cause of every failure may prove to be elusive.

Science (or rather scientists) can be wrong. Two informed experts can view the identical scientific data and reach opposing conclusions. One example is the stock market. For every trade, there is a winner and a loser. Someone sold (or bought) too soon or too late. The law of averages does not require perfection, only a correct decision most of the time.

Most confounding is the curious evolution of science upon receipt of additional information. We were trained in our childhood to brush our teeth with vertical strokes. As an adult, we are instructed to use horizontal strokes to reduce the buildup of plaque. The most difficult thing for a scientist to admit is they made a mistake. Remarkably, many a scientist will fail numerous times before success.

Scientists are not only trained to trust their data, but also evaluate and only utilize relevant data to declare a scientific truth. A scientist will argue the ability to evaluate and use only the relevant data is a fundamental difference between a scientist and a statistician. Many a statistician will encounter one of life's greatest disappointments, "To discover what they thought to be true was not."

Unfortunately, politics has recently exploited our trust in science. While a politician claims we cannot trust other politicians, most claim we should always trust the science (except when they disagree with the outcome). When the politician pledges their trust in science, we feel pressured to pledge trust in the wisdom of the politician to make informed decisions.

The application of scientific principles is universal without regard to the presence of borders. During my military career, we conducted training on "Soviet Awareness" to provide an understanding into the philosophy of our foe. As a mockery to our motto "In God We Trust," the presentation contained a photograph of a Soviet fighter with the assertion that "God does not make the plane fly. Sound engineering principles cause the plane to fly." The Soviet Union no longer exists; nonetheless, the motto for the operational test director for the U.S. Department of Defense is "In God We Trust, all others bring data."

House Arrest during COVID-19

At first, I was taken aback by the attitude of medical professionals. They seemed "giddy" with the potential for a major pandemic. Many prepared their entire career for such an event and had not been able beforehand to contribute to our society. The last pandemic was over 100 years ago. This could be their moment in the sun. Nevertheless, sunshine can be a strong disinfectant.

Given the reality that no battle plan survives the first contact with the enemy, the conflicting direction appeared baffling to the public. Guidance from the Centers for Disease Control and Prevention (CDC) appeared to be a colossal disaster. Do not wear a mask - Always wear a mask - Wear two masks! We have tests - We do not have tests! The virus is not transmitted by contact with surfaces - The virus may be transmitted from surfaces! The inmates from the CDC appeared to be running the asylum. The best professionals in the world only had 100 years to plan and practice.

During my military career, I participated in several responses with a front-row seat for the information provided to leadership. The fog of war (or crisis) always creates uncertainty. Decisions must be made in real time with the best available information. The only certainty is the uncertainty of the information.

In reality, about one-half of the initial reports of an incident have a major error. The time or location may be incorrect; the number and status of injured personnel may be wrong. Updates and corrections to initial reports are expected. The same challenge exists for every crisis including a major pandemic. The integrity of the information is only as good as the source at the time.

An interesting story from my Navy career to demonstrate different approaches to manage uncertainty. The Navy and Marine Corps both report to the Secretary of the Navy. However, the leadership of the two services have different philosophies regarding initial reports. The Navy demands timeliness while the Marine Corps insists on accuracy. As a case in point, the watchstanders in the Navy Operations Center are instructed to immediately notify the chain of command by email with a follow-up phone call and clearly state, "This is an initial report. Amplifying information to follow."

The different approaches may occasionally result in conflict. One example of a triggering incident could be the crash of an F-18. As the Navy and Marine Corps both fly F-18s, the Navy would make an initial report to the Secretary of the Navy while the Marines would wait to verify detailed information, such as the command owning the aircraft and condition of the pilot. When the Marines would eventually call the Secretary of the Navy, he would say, "I know. The Navy told me." The senior Marine from the Marine Corps Operations Center would then call to demand the Navy change their procedure.

In any crisis, the information does change and decisions may need to change based on updated information. The objective of supplying both timely and accurate information to the press and public cannot be perfection as timeliness and accuracy are always in conflict. In a crisis, additional information will likely be received several times a day. Leadership must evaluate the information and make informed - not perfect - decisions. Hindsight is 20/20. With the 24-hour news cycle and a video library with decades of tapes, anyone can challenge an official with a conflicting statement made in the past and demand an explanation.

During an unfolding crisis, trust may be an issue of life or death for both you and your family. In our political system, elected officials are expected to seize a leadership role in a crisis and make informed decisions. The irony is obvious as politicians are always among the "least trusted professions." Creditable surveys find the public trust of politicians is less than 10 percent. In other words, over 90 percent of the citizens do not trust what they say or do.

Given the recognition of the time-critical constraints for action in a national crisis, federal and state legislatures (a group of politicians) have granted the power to take immediate actions to the executive branch (President and state governors, another group of politicians). The outcome is foreseeable. Confusion, mistakes, and contradictions will likely follow. We are left to wonder, "Who is really in charge?"

Few politicians possess the ability to become effective leaders in a crisis - a unique skill set - as they lack the ability to concede a mistake or to revisit a past flawed decision as they are predisposed by nature to deflect every contentious issue. Whereas an effective - maybe even despised - leader must have the ability to tell us to "Go to hell" in such a way that we will look forward to the trip.

Every national crisis has a turning point when the issue transitions to a concern - not a crisis. During an emergency, the inflection point may be identified when one group of politicians begins to criticize the other group of politicians. Thus after the initial phase of the crisis, we are forced to make personal decisions concerning life or death with conflicting information.

During our lifetime we have endured many shutdowns. Most were government shutdowns instigated by one group of politicians. During each shutdown (or snow emergency), the declaration of an essential employee and non-essential employee was promulgated. Throughout my military career, we were declared to be essential employees with a purpose in life. Later as a civilian, I became a non-essential employee, absent an important function in society.

The pandemic has further defined us as to our ability to contribute to our functioning society. Detailed lists with every profession were generated. The non-essential were ordered to "Stay-at-Home" under house arrest as we were regarded not to be of any benefit to the rest of society. Although we could venture outside to purchase food and medicine from the essential ones, we were otherwise restricted to our small units of confinement for 24-hours a day. Even the inmates in solitary confinement are allowed to exercise one hour per day.

As non-essentials under house arrest perplexed by the confusion, mistakes, and contradictions, we should nevertheless feel blessed to have survived another crisis of life; and we may in a bizarre way be thankful for the experience as we will likely in the future be able to fully appreciate our normal boring lives.

Worst of Times

The news of the day is alarming with the nuclear threats, civil unrest, racism, drug addiction, military conflict, and widespread disrespect for authority (police, government officials, teachers, and the military). Are these the worst of times?

The time is not the present day, rather the 1960s. As teenagers in our formative years, we witnessed the Cold War, civil unrest, racism, political assassinations, the drug culture, burning ghettos, the police action in Vietnam, and the National Guard shooting students. Vivid memories from our youth are somewhat diminished with the passage of time, however the 60s were characterized by the extremes - hostile confrontation or complete disengagement as in "Turn on, Tune out." As with most problems in the 60s, it usually got worse before it got better.

The psychologists have a simple explanation, "Each generation is responsible to raise the next generation of barbarians." As such, every generation must attempt to surpass the last in the level of vulgarity and radical confrontation. Given the last few years, there will be little left for the next generation to surpass.

The world of information is much different than in prior decades. The news cycle never slows with 24-hour cable channels with instant updates on websites. Everyone is continuously connected via a hand-held gadget. News of the day (true or false, serious or benign) spreads within minutes stimulating an immediate response of outrage. The actual importance of any news is lost in the rush to inform. We are left to ponder the issue of the day and whether or not it really matters in our lives.

The ramblings of common folks (informed or otherwise) are now empowered with the simplicity of digital communication. Years ago, only a few had a letter to the editor selected to be published. Today, the few are the many with a couple keystrokes.

The really important issues concerning our freedom, opportunity, or pursuit of happiness occur rather infrequently, a few rare events within a lifetime. Nowadays, we are bombarded daily by the prophets of doom and despair.

The world should (and does) change, hopefully for better. Change follows a sequence of three successive stages. First is the fight for recognition, followed by acceptance, then the war for dominance. Every bereaved group believes they will only be truly free when everyone thinks and behaves as them - usually in conflict with the assured freedoms of other groups thereby provoking the expected responses of vulgarity and radical confrontation.

As a barbarian from a prior generation, I may have missed the 60s as I was preoccupied with my golf swing, pretty females, and deer hunting - each demanding my undivided attention at different times. Nevertheless, several vivid memories remain, including respect for authority figures, starting the public school day with a bible reading, and the rewards for hard work. My hopes and dreams were kept alive by looking forward to the next major milestone of life: first job, first car, first date, first kiss, and first love.

In our youth, there were occasional reminders of the bigger world with duck and cover drills, the Vietnam War where 200 young men died each week, and political assassinations. Nevertheless as a child under the legal age, we were responsible only for our behavior and success, normally defined by good grades in school. Although a young man could be drafted into the military at 18 years of age, he could not vote or drink any alcohol until 21. Adult decisions and responsibilities could be deferred until later in life.

Today, our youth are misinformed as to their rights as children (which do not legally exist). As perceived rights come with perceived responsibilities, they are challenged to engage well ahead of normal childhood concerns. Far too many are expected to advocate for adult decisions and instructed to educate their parents (with limited factual context) on the wide variety of political issues, such as a right to a free college education, limitless medical care, and guaranteed income for life. The innocence of youth may be forever lost. The educators (as surrogate parents) are breeding the next generation of barbarians.

On the other hand, the socialistic programs of our generation of barbarians are vulnerable to similar criticism. Medicare and Social Security will be "insolvent" in 8 years and 20 years, respectively. As both programs are "pay as you go" the next generation will bear the burden. Similarly, the national debt numbers in the tens of trillions of dollars, the interest and principal to be paid by following generations.

Let the barbarian games begin. Are these the worst of times?

A Squirrel for Arrow

Three years ago, we invited Arrow into our family. Arrow is a Soft Coated Wheaten Terrier, an all-purpose Irish farm dog. The breed is characterized by its soft flowing gently waving coat. The literature advises, "The Wheaten is a lively, inquisitive, and exuberant dog who jumps up and kisses to express their love for people. Wheatens are a sensitive breed. Puppies must be carefully raised and socialized with gentle, but firm and consistent training." Little did we know our lives would never be the same.

As with any young creature, life is a journey of discovery. Our first day together, Arrow discovered windows with an abrupt bump. The second day, he discovered mirrors (and his reflection) while walking the hallway of our high rise. The doggie in the mirror also seems to enjoy touching noses. Arrow learns quickly, the most intelligent and strong-willed dog we have ever known.

The first year was a unique challenge. As a preview for our future, Arrow bit the instructor in puppy kindergarten drawing blood, but nevertheless graduated with his class of puppies. The second set of classes did not produce any major improvement in behavior. As the breeder previously warned, "If you give him an inch, he will take ten miles." Arrow is definitely the "alpha dog" of the house.

Given his intelligence, Arrow knows he is blessed to be a resident of Leisure World. The open areas, particularly the woods around the golf course, offer a world of odors on every clump of grass, stick, bush, and tree. Arrow sniffs everything. On his walks (four times per day), he enjoys meeting other dogs and interacting with the wildlife in Leisure World.

With the abundance of wildlife, Arrow's hunting skills are tested each day. Deer, geese, rabbits, squirrels, and an occasional fox offer a rich menu to practice his stalking skills. However, squirrels are his favorite quarry. The woods around the Greens are infested with the fluffy critters, a dozen or more sightings are common. Upon sighting, Arrow slowly stalks the target closing the distance until the squirrel moves behind a tree. Seizing the opportunity, Arrow runs around the tree to discover the squirrel has vanished. He seldom looks up to see the squirrel looking down. Undeterred, Arrow locates the next target.

Unfortunately, Arrow understands the days of squirrel abundance may be limited. During the last several years, the tree cutters have been active, removing over a hundred dead trees (the home of the squirrel). Many more trees are (or will be) marked for removal. Every living creature requires suitable habitat to survive - an arrangement of food, water, shelter, and living space. Den trees are the primary shelter for squirrels. Without den trees, there can be no squirrels.

Periods of boom and bust are common in nature. A wildlife species will normally reach carrying capacity before the population is limited by the available habitat, predators, parasites, starvation, weather, accidents, and disease. The removal of den trees creates competition for scarce resources. The squirrel population will eventually succumb, the healthy will likely move away.

The major responsibility for the expected demise of our squirrel population is attributed to poor management, though a better name would be apathy, that is, when folks defer concern and action until the situation is beyond effective treatment requiring drastic action. Although the forests of Leisure World appear from a distance to have a healthy canopy of mature trees, the health of the forest is in rapid decline. Even though all age classes are present, a disproportionate percentage of the trees are in the older age class, likely planted 50 years ago during the early days of Leisure World. Stress and mortality increase with the age of a tree.

A review of the history of our forests is instructive. The old settlers claim a squirrel could travel east from the Atlantic Ocean to the Mississippi River without touching the ground. During the late 1800s and early 1900s, the timber barons marched westward clearcutting the old-growth forests.

The harvest technique of clearcutting (the removal of all trees and vegetation) is also known as even-aged management. Although the new trees may grow at different rates, they are all the same age. Even-aged management allows all seedlings to equally compete for growing space, and thus provides the highest abundance of trees in the future forest. In other words, the forests (which sprouted after the timber barons) do not resemble the old-growth forests. Our eastern forests are different now. Likewise, the current forests in Leisure World are unlike those before the existence of Leisure World.

The social and economic costs to artificially sustain a different forest can be prohibitive. As any natural system is disturbed, the force of nature attempts to restore the ecosystem to its original condition. Mother Nature can be unforgiving to impulsive manipulators. Within the last century, she has raised an army of insects and diseases to recover her old-growth forests. Her arsenal of weapons include: gypsy moths, oak leaf rollers, chestnut blight, elm spanworm, pear thrips, Dutch elm disease, beech bark disease complex, sugar maple decline complex, emerald ash borer, and others.

Similar to a wildlife population, a forest of trees needs diversity to survive. For plants, the principle of biodiversity (too much of any one thing could be harmful) needs the diversity of plant species (different species), the diversity within a plant species (different subspecies), and the diversity of age. As Mother Nature is constantly challenging the status quo, a forest must be diverse to endure.

Our current tree crisis in Leisure World is also complicated by the demise of ash trees from the emerald ash borer. Similar to numerous communities across the country, Leisure World planted too many ash trees 50 years ago. Although the choices from the past were selected with good intentions, few were aware of any long-term consequences. Given the life cycle of trees (70 to 150 years), no one will observe the results of their decisions.

The past is the past - and we can only make informed decisions in the present. However, we appear to suffer from the same apathy as the previous caretakers. The greatest danger to our forest and wildlife populations in Leisure World is the limited reactionary behavior of the caretakers. They only engage in intervention at the beginning of tree life (planting) and end of life (removal). Photos of a hundred dead tree stumps do not contribute to a solution.

A healthy forest to support a healthy squirrel population requires continuous care and nourishment. On average, a forest needs to be thinned every decade or so to provide sufficient space for healthy trees and to allow sunlight to reach the forest floor to stimulate the next generation of healthy trees. Saving a few den trees for squirrels and other wildlife would also be beneficial.

As in the past, some may suggest the simplest action is to allow Mother Nature to take her course, although she will eventually enact her revenge. The option of waiting only ensures further destruction. The damage (current and future) to our forests in Leisure World from apathy is self-imposed.

We, the caretakers of our forests of Leisure World, must provide continuous care and nourishment to ensure our forests are healthy to be enjoyed by the next generation of residents.

Arrow thanks you for your concern.

When I'm 65

Yesterday, I achieved (or rather attained) a significant milestone in one's life. I am now 65 years of age and officially a senior citizen. Although the actual event (my birthdate) was a matter of certainty, my emotions (before, during, and after) could be the foundation of a study in the chemistry of brain molecules for aging human lifeforms.

A long, long time ago when I was 35, a salesman enlightened me with a statistic that a 35-year-old had a 9 in 10 probability of reaching the age of 65. Therefore, I should increase my personal savings to prepare for the future by investing in his family of mutual funds with an 8.5 percent load fee. Another sign of my advancing age is I actually remember mutual funds with such high load fees. Today, all mutual funds are no-load with an annual management fee.

Given such favorable odds of survival to age 65, my life strategy was to accumulate as many financial options as possible. I sacrificed throughout my working career to save for the future to ensure my financial security. The Boy Scout motto of "Be Prepared" applies.

On my last day of work, I began the transition from saving for the future to aging in place with a comfortable lifestyle. Nevertheless, my deeply rooted habits of frugality remain hard to suppress. I currently drive a reliable 20-year-old Toyota Avalon. The arrival of my 65-year milestone has forced me to confront the numerous choices for my remaining years.

Today, I am eligible for a variety of senior discounts and benefits. From tax credits available to Maryland seniors to Medicare eligibility, I am harvesting the fruits of my life of labor. However, my enjoyment appears to be short-lived as I am now the target for phone scammers. The police and IRS are issuing weekly warrants for my arrest.

As a 65-year-old, Medicare is my primary health care insurance supplemented by TRICARE for Life requiring enrollment in Medicare Part B. My previous attitude toward Medicare had been to defer a comprehensive understanding until I became eligible, as if I could somehow postpone the decision or at least not have to think about it. My first waypoint on the Medicare journey occurred three months prior to turning 65 when I became eligible to apply for Medicare. The online application was relatively stress-free. I received my Medicare card in the mail about a month later.

One month later, I received a letter from Medicare declaring my Part B premium (and future premiums), unbeknownst to me, would be higher by several hundred dollars per month due to the Income Related Monthly Adjustment Amount (IRMAA). The letter explained only five percent of Medicare recipients pay the IRMAA, as if I should be delighted to be in such a select group.

Recently, I have become much more sensitive to greetings such as "Sir" and "Old Man." Given my military career, the words should not trigger any negative reaction. As a Naval officer, the term "Old Man" was accepted as a term of respect for experience. I was first referred to as an "Old Man" at age 43. Today, the words induce a different set of emotions. Likewise, I react differently when someone holds a door open.

Somehow as a senior, I sense a loss of respect for our generation. I am somewhat saddened by the ease at which those who prey on the most vulnerable are permitted to operate. With current technology, shutting down the predators is only a matter of will. Nonetheless, the current generation appears to be more obsessed with the rallying cry of "Medicare for All" and to advocate for the release the "non-violent" predators back into our society to target seniors with their next scam. The acceptance in our society for this cruel behavior is distressing. We need to restore accountability to protect our freedoms from fear and harassment earned by our generation.

In any event, I have successfully avoided the high-risk behaviors befalling the other unfortunate 10 percent of my year group. I am a survivor. Now, what do I do? What is the next milestone? Is it 66, 70, 75, 80, 85, or 90? And how do I process my Medicare claims while incarcerated in a federal penitentiary?

About the Author

Before retirement, Woody was educated and served as a Navy nuclear engineer. During 37 years of Naval service, he served in challenging leadership positions and authored tens of thousands of government documents with meticulous precision, each and every word carefully chosen to convey a precise meaning. As great writing lays bare the author's soul, the sterile narratives of technical writing can never be great. He rejects any portrayal as a "good writer" but admits to being the brutal editor, including of his own essays. He currently resides in Leisure World at Vantage Point East. Woody serves as the President of the Writers Group of Leisure World. He has self-published three books.

CHAPTER 12

IMAGES

By Beverly Silverberg

The Move [1]

(Written in 2020 at the beginning of the pandemic)

A pandemic was not one of the contingencies my husband and I considered when we thought about moving. We were looking for a retirement community that offered activities we wanted to pursue such as fitness programs, art classes, a book club, wood shop, and trips to theaters. None of which has happened yet.

I loved the garden in my home, but grew to hate the deer that ate my hosta to the ground and thought the flowers I planted were their salad bar. The maintenance on the house had become onerous and in the weeks before we moved, a gutter sprang a leak, one pipe in the basement required repair and a section of wall needed to be replaced, convincing us that we had made the right decision.

An apartment that was beautifully landscaped, with a number to call if anything failed and no worries about leaf or snow blowing seemed just the right thing for us. Since we moved in four weeks ago, we've barely seen a soul in the halls, in the elevators or on the streets. We take our evening walks with our masks and gloves and paper towels for touching elevator buttons and getting mail.

---

[1] Originally published April 18, 2020, The Washington Post, Real Estate Section.

The few folks that are out are similarly garbed and we wave and give each other a wide berth. I look forward to the day we can meet our neighbors, swim in the pool, eat at the restaurants and not have another box to unpack.

Today marks one month since we moved to Leisure World in Silver Spring. What an adventure! Who imagined we'd move to a retirement community at the beginning of a pandemic whose most vulnerable victims are seniors? Surely not us. But as fate decreed, and we are not fatalists, that's just what we did.

For months before our move we had been giving away, throwing away and selling the possessions we had spent more than half a century accumulating. We had filled our attic, our basement, our two-car garage, a tool shed, four bedrooms, an office, a living room, a dining room, a den, a basement living room, bar, utility room, work benches, laundry room, and a kitchen with "stuff." And now, within a matter of months we needed to dispose of it or move it to a three bedroom apartment. Downsizing is truly daunting!

My husband and I were on a collision course with reality. As many trips as we took to Community Forklift (a non-profit that takes tools and building materials); and to Value Village (a non-profit that takes almost anything in the way of household goods); and the library to donate bookshelves full of books; and to A Wider Circle (a non-profit that takes usable clothing for people needing them); and trips to the hazardous waste disposal, electronic recycle and the dump, we still had a whole lot of "stuff" to get rid of.

For months we'd been selling beloved possessions on our local list serve. What a treasure that community list serve turned out to be! Hubby parted with his barbells, riding mower, his chipper shredder, his snow blower and leaf blowers (yes plural), not to mention his pressure washer, 16' ladder and assorted and sundry tools. He gave all kinds of power tools to his brother-in-law, nephew, son-in-law and neighbors. The chainsaw, rakes, shovels, wheelbarrow, seed spreader and other useful items went to whoever would take them. When you have three workbenches and four tool boxes, there are a lot of tools! Some even came with us. Too many actually, but that's my take.

I meanwhile was stripping three fireplaces of tools and a truly magnificent beaux arts fireplace fan I'd named Minerva. Our niece got one set of fireplace tools and Minerva found an appreciative buyer. Fireplace mantel adornments that were gifts from dear ones or bought on trips to faraway places were painful to just give away or sell. Truth be told, some of them made it to the new apartment that has no fireplace mantels and now must find another home.

Silver, brass, pewter, crystal, vases, mirrors, baskets, Christmas paper, lamps, postcards, greeting cards, 45 rpm records, an espresso machine, ice buckets, furniture, book cases, filing cabinets, rugs and art all found new homes. Since I just couldn't part with the record albums, they came with us, as did a record player. The local elementary school got lots of office supplies. I'm going to miss my Elliot Porter posters of spring and fall and my beautiful print of Georgia O'Keefe's red poppy. Household items were sold, some were given away and other goodies went out the door with the "junk" man, including tables, chairs and the wonderful roll top desk whose dimensions were too big for the folks who expressed an interest in having it. Lawn furniture went along with the grill and patio flower pots to a young couple delighted to have them.

You might ask, why did we do this? We occasionally ask ourselves the same. But it's all our daughter's fault. She looked around our house one day and said, "Mother, you are not allowed to die until you get rid of all this stuff!" We knew she was right. Not fair to burden her with all our things, particularly when she was quick to say she didn't want anything. Not the china, not the silver, not the crystal, not anything. She ended up with the dining room set anyway. It simply would not fit in the apartment and I couldn't bear to give it away, except to her. She's not wholly to blame, however. The stairs and maintenance on a large home finally took their toll.

Well, back to the move. The original estimate for the move was $1,300, the final cost was $2,890. Yes, more than double. Can't blame the moving company really. I do blame them for busting a hole in the wall and breaking some furniture, although every other household item arrived intact. That's because they must have chopped down a forest for the boxes and paper they used to pack everything.

After all the giving away, selling and hauling away we still had five large boxes of framed family pictures, closets of clothes, kitchen dishes, glassware and gadgets, and hubby's tools and wires that he thought he might need, many of which are still in boxes. The movers, when they came and saw what was left to pack immediately called in two extra men (for a total of five) and a total of 47 boxes in addition to several wardrobes and the 30+ boxes we had already packed. We had to get the job done in one day. That was all the elevator time we had from the Leisure World folks. And by the way, we'd been moving things to the apartment for weeks, fragile things like my glassware; valuable things like silverware and irreplaceable things like birth and marriage certificates.

Did I mention all of my mother-in-law's beautiful art work? Approximately 20 oil paintings, collages, and art of various sizes that we inherited when my 98-year-old father-in-law died ten years ago had to come with us to the new apartment. Luckily there are lots of walls. The framed family pictures, however, are an impossible challenge. They are still sitting in a pile staring at us every time we walk by them. For years, some of those pictures graced the piano we were fortunately able to give away, some of them came from our parents' homes when they downsized.

As we began unpacking, we realized what a poor job we had done of divesting ourselves of "stuff"! Did I really need the Keurig my 98-year-old mother had left behind when she moved to my brother's home last year? Our coffeemaker, Melita coffee pot and coffee press were already too much for our little galley kitchen. The large electric frypan was great in our old house, but would I be making potato pancakes for a crowd during Chanukah in our new apartment? Not likely. How about the Teflon coated turkey roaster that could easily handle a 25-pound bird? I should never have brought it to the new kitchen and I'd already given my other roasting pan to my son-in-law. Did I mention the stainless steel poacher? All sitting on a ledge above the cabinets in the kitchen and destined for new homes when the threat of this pandemic ends.

I won't get into the things my spouse could not bring himself to get rid of, but as I look around our office and in the space that houses our little stack washer-dryer, which he has stuffed with the remains of his workbenches, I shudder. Use your imagination. I envision a day when not only is the pandemic over, but our downsizing is done. May they both come quickly!

Is It Worth My Life?

Prologue: We moved to a senior living community on March 12, 2020. COVID 19 caused a shutdown in Maryland on March 15 and seniors were considered one of the most at-risk groups for catching the virus. By July our boxes were unpacked, but our anxiety only increased.

A loaf of bread, a gallon of milk and a dozen eggs, but are they worth my life? Having to make a risk benefit analysis each time I run out of the necessities is my *new normal*, and I hate it. Risk perception is an interesting study. Before COVID 19 struck, people were more afraid of public speaking than flying or dying. People blithely got into their automobiles, although the likelihood of a fatal accident was far greater than being struck by lightning. But now we are forced to reconsider our priorities.

Do we dare go to the supermarket? What if people aren't wearing masks? Why are they touching that tomato without gloves? Did they wash their hands? Perhaps we should use a buying service? That would give a job to someone else who needs it. But what if they're sick? What if they're asymptomatic? How afraid should we be? The questions are endless, the answers are not so forthcoming.

Now as senior citizens, my husband and I are in the highest risk category. Doing a threat assessment each time we need groceries wasn't how we planned to spend our "golden years." Yet, that's where we find ourselves. My husband and I listen carefully to the experts on television. We read reports in the newspapers and on the web. We discuss the latest studies and findings and conclude that there's not enough information to make informed decisions.

This virus is too new, and it's also too deadly to get it wrong. We have friends who are immuno-compromised; we have friends who have tested positive; and we know people who have died. What should we do? Sadly, in this case, expert opinion is not so expert, nor is it consistent. The scientific community is marshaling its resources to gather data, do the analyses and find answers, but it's a slog.

Epidemiologists, infectious disease doctors, researchers, and state and federal health officials cannot yet tell us definitively if the virus is airborne, foodborne, transmitted by letters or packages, contracted by physical contact, or all of the above. They can't tell us how severe our symptoms will be or if we will have symptoms. The experts don't know if once we've had the virus we are safe from another bout. We hope they find out soon, but hope is not a strategy.

How long should a bottle of ketchup or mayonnaise sit in the hall before we can safely put it on a pantry shelf? How long is the virus transmittable on different surfaces? We used to wipe down every bottle, every can and every package with disinfectant wipes before putting them away. It took hours. We still wash all the produce and wipe the frozen packages before storing them in the refrigerator or freezer. Does the freezer kill the coronavirus or does it preserve it? Are we doing it right? Are we at risk from the shopping cart or from the items in our cart or both? Not knowing these things makes it super hard to make informed decisions.

So how do we evaluate risk? Here are the high risk items we've said a definite no to: no to flights, no to cruises, no to trips of any sort by bus, train or subway. These are all clearly high risk and we're avoiding them. We take rides in our car and drive to parks where we can walk in the fresh air, masked, of course. No to bars, no to pools, no to gyms (good thing we decided to keep our weights when we moved), no to movies (except on television), no to any place where people congregate without masks.

No to our favorite restaurants, although we have done carryout on rare occasions, like our 55th anniversary. We took what we thought was a calculated risk. A big no to public restrooms. We have our medications mailed to us and try to avoid the pharmacy whenever possible. Generally, no to doctor and dentist's offices, although my husband did get his teeth cleaned and was impressed at the safety precautions taken. They included scheduling an exact time for his arrival, taking his temperature when he came in, a thorough cleaning of the office before and after his appointment. A technician arrayed in what my husband said looked like a hazmat suit and face shield waited for him and did the cleaning. Thankfully, my husband appears to have survived that encounter without contracting the virus. My doctor's visit was virtual. It worked fine.

Since we have to eat, we considered supermarket trips a necessary risk, but not necessarily low risk. Initially, we did use Instacart for shopping. It was a reliable service. We appreciate the precautions that grocery stores have taken to safeguard employees and customers. Early morning senior hours, mask requirements, social distancing reminders, marking one-way aisles, placing checkout folks behind plastic shields all made us feel a bit safer. Checking the percentage of cases in the zip codes where we were going to shop also gave us some measure of confidence.

We take what we consider reasonable precautions. So now we mask up, we wear gloves, we disinfect whatever we buy and bring into the house. We wash our hands a lot! I never realized how often I touched my face until I was told to stop doing that. We always have a shopping list and race through the store as fast as we can to limit our exposure. Sometimes that means forgetting some of the items we came to buy.

We did take what I considered an unnecessary, but an ultimately satisfying trip to Costco. They also provided early morning hours for seniors. The best part is that they had toilet paper and disinfectant wipes! That was a bonanza almost worth the trip. Getting those items violated all the social distancing rules as people descended on the employees who were bringing the wipes and paper out to the floor.

The packages were gone before the employees could place them on the shelves and pallets.

Even though there was a one package per customer limit, some folks cheated by having the person they were shopping with go through the line with the second package. Obviously, people do what they feel they must. Buying non-perishables in quantity hopefully makes for fewer trips. When he can, my husband does his shopping online. I haven't bought anything but food since we moved. This is not good for the economy or my psyche.

Clearly, there are risks associated with everything. Evaluating the level of risk versus the benefit is a personal calculation that each one of us must make. I decided to join a protest of George Floyd's horrific death under the knee of a policeman. I wanted to be counted among those who understand that no one is safe if all of us are not safe. Whether death comes from a virus or from the hands of the police, I believe it must be acknowledged and fought with all of the resources at our command. So I masked up, wrote my sign saying that "We are all George Floyd" and stood with neighbors I did not know as we stood on Georgia Avenue outside the gates of Leisure World and let the passersby know what an atrocity we felt had been committed. People held up their signs, mostly kept six feet apart and decided the risk of remaining silent was far greater than protesting.

My husband and I have been cooped up in our new apartment for the four months since we moved. Pretty poor timing, but who knew? We haven't hugged our grandchildren or celebrated their birthdays since March. We've missed holidays with family and friends. No Passover Seder for the first time in more than half a century, no Memorial Day or July 4th picnics or barbecues, no visits to museums or movies. No trip to the beach this year with family and friends.

We haven't eaten in a restaurant, we haven't had anyone come to visit. No one has been in our apartment except us. It's depressing. And the saddest part is there is no end in sight.

Having said all that, we do know how fortunate we are. We are alive. We are relatively healthy. And we really hope to stay that way. We have each other. So many others have been hit hard by the double whammy of losing their jobs and having the virus threaten their lives and their families. Their challenges and the stress they are under are unimaginable. We are indebted to all the "essential workers" the nurses, doctors, EMTs, pharmacists, grocery workers, and others who put themselves in harm's way each day they go to work. They have our respect and gratitude.

We are thankful that we can FaceTime and Zoom with family and friends and simply can't imagine how awful life would be without being able to connect, at least electronically. We wear our masks and gloves when we go for a walk in the evenings. We rarely see other people and when we do we give each other a wide berth and wave hello. Someday, we hope to actually get to know some of our new neighbors and see more of their faces than their eyes. We hope to visit the gym and swim in the pool and play bridge, eat out and go to a real theater. But in the meantime, we assess the risks of daily living. We shop for milk, bread and eggs, we give each other haircuts, we buy large quantities of food at each supermarket visit and are grateful we can. And we pray for this pandemic to end.

Epilogue: We know much more today than when this was written in 2020. However, although restrictions have lifted somewhat, the virus spreads with new variants attacking people. The unvaccinated are still dying and the American death toll exceeds one million. The pandemic is a national tragedy of dreadful consequence.

How We Discovered a Passion for Pickleball

THWAK! THWAK! Followed by moans and groans and WHOOPS and cheers. My husband and I, who were on our daily walk of discovery, looked at each other and followed the sounds to the courts behind Clubhouse II at Leisure World (LW). We were invited in with smiles and encouragement and were told that folks were playing something called "Pickleball." At first glance they looked like tennis courts, but not. Nets and courts are smaller and the most common game is doubles. That's not the only difference. There are some interesting rules, like staying out of the "kitchen" an area on either side of the net. But those rules are easy to master as is the game and scoring.

Pickleball combines parts of tennis, badminton, and ping pong. It is played with paddles and plastic balls with between 26 to 40 holes like a whiffle ball. The thwacking sound was coming from the paddles hitting the ball. The moans and groans from the players missing a shot, the cheers from players getting in a winning shot.

Pickleball grew in 2021 to almost five million players, according to the 2022 Sports and Fitness Industry Association. Fifty-two percent of players are 55 or older. We watched for a while, talked to some of the players and came back to watch some more. It looked like fun, so we decided to buy some paddles and try it ourselves. It was fun! We used to play tennis, but we found pickleball to be easier on the body. LW has both indoor and outdoor courts. We've found players to be a very hardy lot, playing even when the temperature dips into the 30s.

If you never heard of pickleball, and I hadn't, that's because it was invented in 1965 by three dads finding new ways to entertain their teenage kids. NBC News called it: "the fastest growing sport you've never heard of." There's been a 650 percent increase in the number of players in the last six years. It now has a professional component with TV contracts and endorsements. You can watch tournaments on YouTube and CBS Sports Network has broadcast National Pickleball championships.

We are not aspiring to play at that level. We wanted a bit of exercise, a bit of fun and not a lot of pressure. We got all that and more. A big bonus was that we got to meet other residents. Because of the pandemic we had met virtually no one since we moved to Leisure World in March of 2020. Now we were becoming regulars on the courts where people are generally more than six feet apart and feeling somewhat safe from COVID exposure.

One of the rules I really like is the one about not berating another player for missing a shot and more importantly, making it a point to congratulate a player for making or even almost making a good shot. Pickleball is a game that has a lot of strategy and skill associated with it. You know the line about "practice makes perfect"; well no question, we won't get perfect, but practicing to improve our game is fun. Try it! You'll probably like it!

The Cruise from Hell

Prologue 1994: It is January and winter simply won't let go. Old man winter is determined to make every person living in Maryland wonder why they are still living there.

As we watch the last patches of snow covering the hardy, optimistic and early crocuses that announce that spring is not too far behind, some of us may daydream about going on a cruise. As we shiver from piercing winds, fond pictures of the Love Boat come to mind. The image of happy, smiling faces basking in warm climes, going from one exotic port to another, gorging on gourmet feasts, are alluring. But let me tell you what the cruise ads don't say. The daydream can turn into a nightmare even when the food is fabulous, the service is spectacular and the ship is beautiful.

My story will never make the travel section of any newspaper. Those folks want you to do what we did when we got so sick of the worst winter in recent memory. My husband Bob and I called a travel agent and said: "Get us out of here. We want to go someplace warm, wonderful, warm, fun, warm." The travel agent got the message and booked us on a new ship the M.V. Royal Majesty.

The slick brochure, with all the pretty pictures, declared "She's a quarter of a billion dollar venture designed for individuals." What could be more appealing? After all, I'm an individual. I just had a major milestone in my life occur, turning the corner on the half century mark. And if that were not enough, my father-in-law was going to turn 85, which really made me feel a lot better about turning fifty. After all, he was in great shape and could outwalk me on a five mile hike hands down. We were going to take him on this cruise to celebrate his milestone, as well as mine and then decided my mom ought to have this wonderful cruise experience too.

The brochure invited me to do anything or nothing; that sounded great. I liked the idea of doing anything, and nothing sounded pretty good also. I made a mental note to try the ancient Tai Chi meditation at sunrise, take some dance lessons, play bridge, and soak in the hot tub. I was game to try most anything. I did none of the above.

The brochure shows epicurean delights "creatively and masterfully planned." It also promised special diets "for healthy appetites." Not meaning healthy as huge, but healthy as in concerned about calories, sodium and cholesterol. Clearly, this was something I wanted to take advantage of, or so I thought.

The advertised theater, music, entertainment, and comedians all sounded like fun. Even karaoke was promised, with hundreds of songs and lyrics available for the exhibitionists willing to let others in the audience snicker or admire, depending on their ability to carry a tune. Since Bob has told me often enough that I couldn't carry a tune if it were strapped on my back, I knew karaoke was out for me, but there was so much else to do.

Wow, was I ready for this cruise. The weather in Maryland was awful. I told everyone how much I was looking forward to getting away with Bob and how neat it would be to have my mom and father-in-law along. They all said how lucky I was, how much fun I was going to have and how jealous they were. Little did they or I know that in fact they were lucky not to be going where I was headed.

We left from the Baltimore-Washington International Airport on January 29th, after experiencing some of the coldest days of the century. We arrived in Florida to sunshine and 80-degree weather. We took off our down jackets and smiled as we basked in the sunshine.

On January 31, we went to Miami and boarded our cruise ship. The crew was very well organized. Our luggage was taken from us at curbside and our suitcases were delivered to our rooms. We were greeted and had our pictures taken as we boarded the beautiful, gleaming 33,000-ton vessel. There were 1,200 passengers, "snow birds" from Canada and cold cities across the nation and 500 staff, from the Captain and the cruise director to cabin stewards and croupiers in the casino.

We were welcomed aboard, found our cabins, commented on how "compact" and yet fully equipped they were and then went on a tour of the ship. On the Majesty Deck the Calypso Duo were making happy sounds and some guests were already in the pool and hot tub. I was impressed at how quickly some folks dove into the available activities. If the Caribbean beat was not to your liking, there was the choice of a piano bar on the Countess Deck or a six string guitar in the Polo Club on Duchess Deck. People boarded from about 1:00 to 3:30 p.m. For those wanting to eat, a beautiful welcome aboard buffet lunch was available at the Cafe Royale.

At three, there was a briefing on the upcoming ports of call. I decided that I wanted to visit a Mayan ruin billed as the "mysterious walled city of temples set high atop a stunning cliff overlooking the majestic crystal blue Caribbean Sea." Sounded inviting to me, so I signed up for the Tulum and Xel-Ha excursion. Tulum was the first stop, an ancient Mayan site and Xel-Ha, the second stop of the day, was a lovely lagoon, where you could swim or watch the multi-colored fish in the marine park.

The day of our departure from Miami was beautiful. We had a mandatory life boat drill at 4:00 p.m. and everyone walked around in their flotation devices, feeling foolish and hoping we would never again hear the seven short blasts followed by one long blast calling all passengers to their "muster stations." People were all in a good mood and smiling as they listened to the explanations of what to do, where to go and who to follow to get in the lifeboats. The inevitable Titanic jokes were exchanged and then the drill was over.

We watched the Miami skyline disappear as we were escorted out of the port by a tug and looked forward to our exciting voyage. We had a Sailaway Celebration, partied on deck, ate pizza, met some of the other passengers and before we knew it, it was time to get ready for dinner. Our early sitting was in The Epicurean Restaurant and we arrived promptly at 6:00 p.m.

We met our Maître D', our waiter and our busboy and introduced ourselves to the other two couples seated at our table. One couple was from Philadelphia, the other from upstate New York. One man ran a Montessori School, the other was a cattle broker. The wives worked with their husbands. Dinner was delicious. Appetizers, soups, entrees were all tempting, well prepared and then there was dessert; it defied description. So far, so good.

After dinner, there was the choice of dancing to the fabulous Royal Fireworks Band, watching a show, the sing-along karaoke, snowball jackpot bingo and, of course, the casino. For those, who wanted to dine and dance the night away, both were available. The midnight buffet featured Italian dishes and the Royal Court Orchestra was playing in the Palace Theatre. The show we saw featured surprisingly good talent. We enjoyed the entertainment, watched people lose money in the casino, added our contribution and realized we weren't going to make it to the midnight buffet. So we went to bed and stayed there too late to get to Tai Chi at sunrise, although that was one of the things I really wanted to do.

Tuesday was billed as the "At Sea" day and evening dinner attire was to be formal. The morning schedule had a suggested meeting with the fitness director for pump it up aerobics. I liked the sound of that, but somehow after a full breakfast it didn't feel like such a good idea anymore. The waves and consequent rolling of the ship were beginning to get to me.

It's not as if I hadn't come prepared. I had bought wrist bracelets designed to keep me from getting seasick. Don't ask me how they work. I only know they do, or at least thought so when I was on the Chesapeake Bay. Maybe I did not get the right bracelets for the Caribbean Sea. I had wrapped the bracelets around, attached the Velcro snugly and believed that I would not succumb to seasickness. I noticed that others had Dramamine patches behind their ears aimed at warding off the same demons. Neither seemed to work. There were a lot of queasy guests aboard. I took a nap and found being in the horizontal position helped a lot. I spent a lot of time in that position during the cruise.

We dressed for dinner that night. My prime rib was perfectly done. I congratulated myself for avoiding the crème brule. I determined to keep that dinner where it belonged, in my stomach. We went to the show after dinner and laughed at the antics of the juggler, tapped our feet to the rhythm of the musical numbers, enjoyed the comedian teasing the audience and realized that we were not going to make the midnight tropical fruit buffet. I had to be up at the crack of dawn to catch the launch to shore.

It was a glorious orange sunrise. Those of us who had signed up for touring the Mayan ruins were taken ashore at Playa del Carmen on the mainland of Mexico. Bob went with the scuba diving group to Palancar Reef in Cozumel and our folks decided to walk around the city, see the sites and shops at their own pace. The day was perfect for scrambling over, around and through the ruins of Tulum. The guide, a descendant of the Mayans of the region, gave an inspired recital of Mayan history, culture and gossip. It felt good to be in the sunshine and on solid ground. I hooked up with Bob in Cozumel, we shopped and got back on the ship. Our folks were waiting to hear about our adventures.

Wednesday night was when the storm hit. We were lucky we had dinner at the early seating, because the glasses didn't start to fall off the tables until the second one. The silverware flew out of drawers, but it didn't matter because no one felt hungry at that point. We went to the show and the comedian was holding onto her microphone for dear life. That turned out funny because the microphone wasn't anchored any more than she was. As she swayed back and forth, she quipped, "I'm from California, I should be used to this." That got a big laugh.

My mother was feeling as badly as I was, and the pills weren't helping. She thanked me for inviting her to share the experience, but suggested she'd pass on the next cruise. The guys seemed not to have inner ears because they were not affected, lucky them. I knew this was another night I wouldn't make the midnight buffet and this one was billed as The Royal Banquet, complete with ice sculptures. I was disappointed.

I went back to the cabin and lost my dinner. It was much better the first time I tasted it. I fell back on the bed and vowed never to take another cruise as long as I lived, if I lived. I couldn't believe I had paid all those bucks to be so sick. The storm raged all night and I could feel us rocking and rolling, but I tried not to think about it. I just couldn't wait until the next day when we would get to Key West. The thought of dry land sustained me through the night.

Imagine my disappointment when the Captain got on the intercom to tell us that because of the storm and the fifteen-foot waves, he had had to change speed and we weren't going to make Key West at all. We had another day "At Sea." I tried to get some fresh air, but that meant looking at the water going up and down and my stomach did the same. I went to the cabin, took another pill and got back in bed.

By evening, I felt well enough to dress and join the family for dinner. The silverware was back in the drawers and the glasses stayed where they were put. We all agreed that the ship was very nice, the staff was totally service-oriented, the entertainers, when they weren't sick, were quite good, but my vacation did not live up to my expectations. The show that night was called "Unforgettable" and my experience certainly was. I liked the wonderful show tunes and I finally made it to a midnight buffet, but this dream cruise had become a nightmare. And the next time I celebrate a milestone event in my life, you can bet it won't be aboard a ship. Getting there is not half the fun when you're on the Cruise from Hell.

Epilogue 2022: I kept my solemn oath never again to go on a cruise ship for 10 years. Finally, my husband talked me into the Inland Passage to Alaska. I desperately wanted to see the glaciers before they melted away and my husband assured me we would not encounter high seas on the way. He was right and I loved Alaska and the cruise experience. We have had many other wonderful cruises since then, even going back to the Caribbean many times when old man winter revisited us. The COVID pandemic has put what I hope is a temporary halt to our cruising life. We can't wait for it to be safe again to continue our adventures.

Reflections

(For my Grandchildren Mia and Owen)

I long to be profound.
I want to leave my family wise thoughts and helpful insights.
But sadly I fail them and myself.
All I have are my reflections.
Nothing original here.

They must already know how much I love them.
I know I've told them. I know I've showed them.
I've cuddled and kissed them, while I could.
Of course they're much too grown for that now.
The occasional hug will have to do.

Can I help them to see how lucky they are to be healthy?
Of course not, we take health for granted until it's gone.
Can I help them to see how their lives are blessed?
Of course not, they've always had life's blessings.

Can I spare them painful experiences?
Of course not, we seem to learn only from our own mistakes.
We only appreciate the absence of pain, once we've known it.
And sadly, painful lessons are the most indelible and memorable.

What can I share with you my darlings on the threshold of your lives?
Will it help if I tell you to live your lives fully and with love; or will
  you wonder what that means?
Can I tell you to be mindful and kind and that these traits are gifts
  that will repay you tenfold?
Shall I remind you that "thank you" and "please" are always welcome
  words?

I'm sure you already know not to hurt anyone's body, spirit or heart.

If what you're doing is important to you, keep trying.
Be willing to fail until you succeed.
Remember don't defeat yourselves by not trying.
Believe in yourselves, as I believe in you.
Be confident! Be honest! Be steadfast!

Make good friends and know how to be one.
Cherish your family and your relationships.
Find a mentor and be a role model.
Give a helping hand to others.

Care about people and the world around us.
Leave the planet a better place than you find it.
No, there's nothing original here.
Only my reflections and a blueprint for a life worth living.

Seder Without Dad [2]

I can't remember a Passover Seder service when Dad was not sitting at the head of the table.

As a young child, I would help my mother prepare for the week of Passover. We would clean all of the kitchen cabinets; pack up the everyday dishes, pots and pans; and give away the foods that were forbidden: beans, rice, bread and other leavened products. Mom's energy seemed endless as she scrubbed and then relined shelves with clean, white paper and put traditional foods and dishes in the sparkling cabinets.

I loved setting the table for the Seder meal. My parents' red glass dishes were so vivid against the white damask tablecloth. Each place setting had a crystal drinking and wine glass ranging in color from

[2] Originally published April 11, 1990, The Washington Post.

pale rose to deep blue. I always made sure the deep blue glass was at my place.

During the early years of our marriage, my husband Bob and I would travel to my parents' home in New Jersey for the Seder. Bob's folks would come, my younger brother and assorted friends and relatives would all be there. Mom would prepare the "gefilte" fish and her super horseradish (guaranteed to clear your sinuses instantly), golden chicken soup with light and fluffy "knaydlach" (dumplings) and a turkey and pot roast, in addition to assorted vegetables and special Passover "kugels" (casseroles).

And Dad would preside.

Even when the Seder service was moved to our home in Maryland, and we were joined by my brother's family and various friends, Dad would sit at the head of the table and begin with the traditional blessing. He and the Passover Seder were made for each other. The Seder is when the head of the Jewish family reminds all who are gathered at the table how precious freedom is, how freedom cannot be taken for granted, how the Jewish people were once slaves in the land of Egypt, how that slavery came to an end when the Lord sent the ten plagues to convince Pharaoh to free the slaves and let them leave Egypt. And the final plague was the Angel of Death who slew all of the firstborn children, but passed over the Jewish slaves' homes. It is an ancient tale of triumph and survival over great odds.

As I contemplated Passover without Dad and the story of the Exodus being told by someone else, I recalled my parents' personal exodus. They married on April 2, 1942, in Poland. They saw friends and family separated, transported and later learned of their deaths in concentration camps. The young couple stayed ahead of the German armies, spending weeks on trains, crossing borders by night and worrying how they would ever reunite with their relatives. With most they never did. Dad never saw his mother or his youngest brother again. His father did not survive the war, part of the unfathomable figure of 6 million Jews killed in Europe. I was born in 1944, and I apparently added a new dimension of joy and fear to their lives. I'm told I was almost suffocated one night as my parents and their friends crossed a border and worried that my cries would be heard by nearby guards.

After several years in a displaced persons camp in Germany, my parents and I came to America on May 30, 1949, to begin a new life in Passaic, New Jersey. My father's uncle arranged an apartment for us and provided a job for my father, requirements for immigration.

We found personal freedom and in my dad's lifetime. He saw the struggles of Balkan states for freedom and the exodus of hundreds of thousands of people seeking their way to democracy. We listened to Vaclav Havel of Czechoslovakia speak to a joint session of Congress of "former slaves and former masters" creating a new order. Years later, history repeats and it is Volodymyr Zelensky protecting democracy from the Russians in the Ukraine.

As we sat at the Seder table in the year 1990, we contemplated the Seder plate and sampled the symbolic foods on display. We brought the lesson of so many thousands of years ago to its modern analogy. The hard-boiled egg represents life itself. The bitter herbs (grated horseradish) symbolize the bitterness of slavery. The "charoseth" a combination of chopped nuts, grated apples and wine flavored with cinnamon and sugar represents the mortar used by the slaves during construction of Pharaoh's monuments. The greens such as parsley, watercress or celery, symbolize new growth, hope and redemption. They are dipped twice in salt water, which some believe represents tears and others see as symbolic of the parting of the Red Sea leading the way to freedom. A roasted shank bone commemorates the paschal sacrifice which each family brought to the temple in ancient days.

The "Afikomen" is one of three matzahs (unleavened bread) placed separately in the folds of a napkin or matzah cover. The matzah symbolizes the bread of affliction the Jewish slaves ate. It is also a symbol of the great haste in which the Jews fled from Egypt, having time only to bring with them unleavened dough.

Four cups of wine are drunk during the Seder service, and a special cup is placed in the center of the table which is filled at the end of the meal for the coming of the prophet Elijah, symbolizing the hope for a more perfect world of justice and joy for humanity.

My father, Henry Rabner, died on March 19, 1990 at the age of 69. My mother Ann Rabner died on November 6, 2021 at the age of 99. I miss their presence at our Seder table. As the story of bondage and freedom is told once more, it is still hard to accept that Dad's bondage from his sickness was finally over at the unbearable cost of losing him. His two-and-a-half year battle with cancer was finished and he was, in a sense, "free at last."

Each year when we celebrate our physical liberation from slavery, we celebrate also our spiritual freedom when we say the traditional Jewish blessing "Blessed art thou, Lord, King of the Universe, who preserved us and sustained us and brought us to this season."

But now that I'm an orphan, Passover can never be the same.

Ukraine

Incomprehensible what humans do to one another.
With our last breaths we cry out for our mother.

Killing is madness; here or half a world away.
Wantonly extinguishing lives and livelihoods, barbarians hold sway.
Isn't power over part of the planet enough?
Does expansion and mindless destruction prove you are tough?

Of course murder is not new; it was Abel that Cain slew.
Brother slaying brother from the creation of time.
In every country, in every age, exists this shocking crime.
Only the weapons improve.

Have we learned nothing?
How the innocent suffer unknowing why.
They had family, food, shelter and clothing,
All gone in the blink of an eye.

From the ancient Mesopotamians, Egyptians, Chinese, and Romans
To modern Asians, Rwandans, Bosnians and Germans.

Is it always us vs. them? Apparently so.
Americans asunder full of grief and woe.
Now Ukrainians join that never-ending list
That sadly continues to grow.

The ceaseless conflicts leave a trail of broken bodies, broken cities,
  broken hearts.
Is it not enough to fight disease, poverty or climate change?
Why must we fight each other?
How do we stop brothers from killing brothers?
Perhaps more leaders should be mothers.

Friends

I miss seeing your face; I miss hearing your voice;
  I miss you my dear friend.
We used to talk and laugh and play; sadly, all that has gone away.
I see you in my mind's eye; I hear you in my dreams;
  I miss you my dear friend.

So precious was our time together; visits as unpredictable as weather.
But each time we met was as if we'd just parted;
  our conversations quickly restarted.
We thought those moments were endless; but no, now I'm friendless.

My heart is heavy with your loss; my mind replays our meetings.
What I would give to once more hear your cheerful greetings.

I miss seeing your face; I miss hearing your voice;
  I miss you my dear friend.
We used to talk and laugh and play; sadly, all that has gone away.
I see you in my mind's eye; I hear you in my dreams;
  I hold you in my heart; I miss you my dear friend.

Images

What do you see in the mirror?

Is it the five-year old refugee?

A small female phoenix rising from the Holocaust's ashes?

Do you see the teen-age student rushing to classes feeling the weight of survivor's expectations?

Do you see the exultant 21-year-old graduate and young wife on the brink of an unknowable future?

Who do you see in the mirror?

Is it the fretful parents of a beautiful baby girl, doubting the wisdom of bringing another human onto an overburdened planet?

Perhaps you see the naïve 30-year-old dreamer poised to make the world a better place

With no pending plan to accomplish that lofty aim?

The decades fly, a career in public service goes by.

The world is not a better place, how disappointing.

Does the mirror reflect a strong, capable woman, leading the way for other women to succeed on once male-dominated terrain?

Does the mirror show the challenges, struggles,

Accomplishments, and pain?

Only if you see beneath the lines now accenting

The once unlined face, body and soul.

Does the image die with the woman reflected in the mirror or is it engraved in genes, etched in the marrow, or eternally entombed?

What do you see in the mirror?

Only reflections, only images of a moment in time.

About the Author

Beverly Silverberg and her parents survived the Holocaust in Europe and immigrated to America in 1949 after two years in a displaced persons camp in Germany. Fast forward 16 years and Beverly was a lecturer, trainer, and author committed to public service. For a half century, she spent her time creating, developing, and administering successful communications campaigns, first at the U.S. Department of Transportation in the 1970s and then for the Washington Metro for a decade in the 1980s. Afterwards, she formed her own consulting firm specializing in crisis communications. She trained private sector executives and public officials to speak effectively in public and to engage the media positively.

Always advancing the cause of women in the workplace, she worked with federal, state, and local governments on improving their strategic communications and public outreach programs until her retirement. Through the years, Beverly chaired a number of non-profit boards and served as President of the College Heights Estates Homeowner's Association, but her greatest sense of joy comes from her husband, her family, and her two grandchildren.

CHAPTER 13

OUR TIMES

By Paula Lipman

Friendship

You brighten up my darkest day
My problems simply melt away
You add sparkle to my dullest hours
Like a burst of starlight showers.

You appear so kind and caring
When wit and wisdom you are sharing
In my wildest fantasy
You will someday be fond of me.

Our cultural differences revealing
Make you so much more appealing
I wonder if we would have a chance
For a deep friendship or romance.

For now, I will simply smile and chat
And contemplate much more than that.

The Saga of
William Jefferson Clinton

Oh Bill Clinton you're in a sorry mess.
Oh Bill Clinton she should have washed the dress.
Is it any wonder you never have confessed?
Oh Bill Clinton where will you go from here?

Oh Bill Clinton will you be impeached,
That's the conclusion many congressmen have reached.
The country's pardon on TV you have beseeched.
Oh Bill Clinton where will you go from here?

Oh Bill Clinton you're feeling so contrite,
You promised to control your sexual appetite.
Oh Bill Clinton where will you go from here?

Oh Bill Clinton life can be so cruel,
Monika Lewinski has made you quite the fool.
Can you run the country shape up and play it cool?
Oh Bill Clinton where will you go from here?

Oh Bill Clinton we the people wish you well,
Kenneth Starr has made your life a living hell.
What will be the verdict only time and luck will tell?
Oh Bill Clinton where will you go from here?

Trumped

The Republican Party has grown quite sizable
And behaved in a manner unrecognizable.

Our moderate senators have defected
For fear of not being reelected.
Giuliani, Trump's advisor, has taken the rein
And interfered with the government in the Ukraine.

Trump broke the law to discredit Biden.
He's surrounded by sycophants he can confide in.

Trump seems to be on a continuous roll
To defy ethical standards he has sold his soul.
Power at all costs is his ultimate goal.

John Bolton and witnesses can give information
That may lead to trump's incarceration.
Mitch McConnell so I've heard
Has made compromise a dirty word and good government utterly
absurd.

The Democratic Party must make a selection
That would defeat Trump in the Presidential election.

Insurrection

Trump supporters at his will,
radically stormed Capitol Hill.
Right Wing mobs came from all directions,
causing a violent insurrection.
They broke windows causing fights
and trashed everything in sight.
Unmasked mobsters attacked police,
causing mayhem to increase.

Death and injuries came after,
resulting from this dire disaster.
Our country was taken unaware
of this violence to prepare.
Under our laws there is a reason
to label this an act of treason.
Our president should be tried and jailed.
The American people he has failed.
Public opinion has quickly risen,
to put the worst offenders all in prison.
The alt-right fringe's conduct has been erratic
to behave in ways so undemocratic.
Our House and Senate must heal the strife
that threatens our civilized way of life.

The Ukraine

Vladimir Putin is insane
To wage war against the Ukraine.

Russian attacks have been intense
This defies reasoning and common sense.

Many are fleeing this great nation
Giving up homes and occupations.

Journalists have found
That hunger and injuries abound.

Communities have been obliterated
By bombs and weapons as anticipated.

The U.S. and Europe must take heed
To support Ukraine in its time of need.

All democracies must so clearly see
That Ukraine wants to remain independent and free.

It's a frightening revelation
That Putin strives for world domination.

Freezing financial assets in Western banks
Will not prevent Russian missiles and tanks
From causing inhuman devastation
To a democratic nation.

United we must turn the tide
To arrest Putin for war crimes and genocide.

The Supreme Court

Justice Ginsburg had reached great heights
As a champion for women's rights.

She strongly advocated pro-choice
And made sure women had a voice.

Women now encompass law firms and corporations
And all "once only" men's vocations.

Ginsburg fought for justice for minorities, immigrants, the disabled
So their rights to housing, education, and fair salaries would not be
tabled.

No longer do women need male signatures for credit or loans from
the bank
This took a long time to pass, and we have RBG to thank.

Our president will put up a tough fight
To select a Supreme Court justice on the Far Right.

Amy Coney Barrett fits the mold
She's an ultra-conservative of the Opus Dei fold.

The grounds are secretly being laid
To overturn Roe vs. Wade.

The Affordable Care Act is assuredly fated
Under Amy Barrett to be terminated.

There is not a shred of doubt
That insurance, many will be without.

The Court's ratio of Liberals to Conservatives would be three to six
And this is a very dangerous mix
It puts human rights in a terrible fix.

Moral justice must prevail
Or our democratic government will surely fail.

Abortion

Insidious plans are being laid
To overturn Roe v Wade.
Extremists feel women should have no voice
To practice freedom of their choice.

Self-righteous fanatics are bent on banning
All evidence of family planning.

It is an undemocratic distortion
To deny women the right to an abortion.

Arkansas, Texas, and Oklahoma too
Have bid abortion rights adieu.

Southern states without fail
Will throw recalcitrant doctors into jail.

It is a frightening revelation
That courts attack one half of our population.

Budget Woes

Balance the budget
Lower the debt
That's what they tell us
The goal must be met.

We Americans must do our share
To eliminate welfare, health care, and Medicare.
Our great strong industrious nation
Can do without Metro and education.

Hear ye people here's the facts
We would never raise your tax.
Our defense budget remains unscathed
In highest glory it is bathed.

Let's go on a spending spree
One SDI or MX, maybe three.
Americans look up with pride
Remember God is on your side.

Cut aid to theater, arts, and dance
For space programs to advance.
Our OMB shouts out with glee
Let's RIF a government agency.

DOC, DOE, and HHS
Why that makes three.
Medical research slice those costs
Cancer funding can be tossed.
Libraries too are under scrutiny
Not to ax book budgets would amount to mutiny.

Gulf, Exxon, and GE
Are subsidized by you and me.
Taxing them would create a rupture
In the giant corporate structure.

Our priorities have been changed
The balancing act is rearranged.

Global Warming

It is tragic and alarming
The damage caused by global warming.
Flooding, fires, and severe drought
Are wiping entire villages out.

Hurricanes and heavy storms,
Now occur in many forms.
Climate change is here to stay.
We can't make it go away.

Slowing the destruction can be doable
If we rely on energy that is renewable.
Fracking underground for gas
Pollutes the environment alas.
Pipelines dug for fossil fuel are
No exception to the rule.
In Greenland and Antarctica it's not so surprising
Ice caps are melting and the sea level is rising.

Many creatures great and small
Are dying off as I recall.
Plants and animal species in sync
Will soon I fear become extinct.

As humans we must not hesitate
To make changes before it is too late!

Celebration

Fall has arrived the leaves are ablaze
We slowly return to our old ways.
Theaters, concerts, movies, shows
Have opened for how long no one knows.

We shop, dine out, and visit friends
And hope the masking mandate ends.

235

But for now, we should cover our faces
This applies to all ages, nationalities, and races.

Travel can still be a danger
If we sit near an unmasked stranger.
The holidays will soon commence
We must heed old fashioned common sense.

We sing, dance, and dine with joyful cheer
And celebrate the future year.
It would be indeed a triumph too
If COVID-19 disappeared in 2022.

♦ ♦ ♦ ♦ ♦

About the Author

Paula retired after a rewarding career as a law and legislative librarian for the U.S. Department of Energy. Previously, she spent three years as an elementary school librarian in the District of Columbia.

In the 1990s, Paula began writing humorous muse, political, and social satirical poems; and personal romantic poems. Motivated by contentious political debates, she began writing biting commentaries criticizing political agendas, including Congress and the U.S. Supreme Court.

Her interests include live plays, concerts, reading, travel, dining out, and socializing with friends. Before the COVID pandemic, Paula volunteered to tutor second graders in a reading and language arts program sponsored by the Heyman Interages Center of Montgomery County.

She thoroughly enjoys the Writers Group of Leisure World.

CHAPTER 14

THOUGHTS

By Viola Stendardi

Recovering

Even on the worst of days
We have our sunny, upbeat optimists,
Those loving, caring, wise individuals
Who can better tolerate and absorb the
Bitter news, no matter how or why it appears.

Some of us have been feeling the stillness
Of a world grown thin.
Memories sweep by, sadness and
Dissipated joys, those close to our hearts
Having suffered like everyone.

And now, to gratefully accept that
Many have recovered,
Some not needing care any longer,
Ready with feet planted on earth once again.

What beneficence!

Shall we make a deal with destiny,
And gracefully enjoy what we have in the present?

An Unnamed Friend

With all the snow—overnight at least 10 inches
And no sidewalks anywhere in this town,
Only one option exists for my daily walk:
An enormous, well-paved parking lot
Appended to the school athletic field
Almost always vacant these days
Unless a rare game is on the roster.

I have taken possession of this vast unused space
And created a walkway of sorts that meanders
Around its outer perimeters and forms a track.
I walk it most afternoons.

Soon there were more walkers,
Glad for the sharing of good, clean air.
One became my best unnamed friend.
He walked every day, like I,
Dressed completely in black and
With his hands clasped behind his back,
Offering an occasional nod of his head.

As sunlight slanted onto our track
Through the field Pavilion,
It created strange, long shadows that he
Appeared to blend into and shift with
As he rounded the track and
Moved into and out of its bends and curves.

My eyes never left him.
He became my man in black –
The guy who always walked with hands
Behind his back.

The pattern continued for many days.
No changes.
I still walked with eyes glued to scouring the track
In search of my special friend,
Until, at some point, realizing that he was not there at all.

Another day the same,
And another.
Could I sense his presence?
His spirit?
Hardly,
But what, then?

The power of memory finally kicked in
Enough
To be able to see that caring –
Perhaps even loving – was often not enough.

Ode to a Man

The air is quiet and still,
He is gone.
Not a dash of himself
To remind me,
Except in my thoughts
And in my heart—
Nothing in what I see each day
Or find in my shrinking soul
Of the wondrous days just past
Made happy for me by the
Presence of this Man.

Together

I've seen them at the corner
Almost every week, it seems,
Walking, holding hands,
But noticeably sad.

Not unlike today,
When they reached the corner,
Stopping there,
Next to each other,
Thoughtful but hardly speaking.

Perhaps exchanging private feelings?
Nodding every so often,
A quiet glance toward each other,
Gentle, sweet, loving.

The cab arrives –
She gathers her things,
Bag and laptop,
And drifts into the cab.

Settling herself into a seat within reach,
Ready to accept, once again,
The feeling of dreary aloneness,
She happens to look up
And he is there, near her window,
Waving and offering his
Smile of encouragement.

Forgiveness

Forgiveness, an elusive gift
Not ordinarily proffered,
Can appear as unexpectedly
And as amazingly resplendent
As the sun that follows
A southern rainstorm;
But, unlike the sun,
We can seek it out
And, if found, happily
Remember the power
Of its generosity.

Adrift

The kind man who walks
Beside me
Is known to speak with his
Heart.
He disavows misfortune in
Any circumstance
And holds to his fundamental
Regard for patience, goodness and grace.

♦ ♦ ♦ ♦ ♦

About the Author

Viola received a Bachelor of Arts from the State University of New York. During her professional career, she was employed for 25 years as a Secretary and Office Manager for a New York City law firm.

She completed several courses in Creative Writing at New York University and has been awarded Certificates of Recognition by Essex County, New Jersey, in the Legacies Writing Contest for 2013 and 2016.

She also completed courses in Memoir Writing by instructor Lisa Romeo, teacher in a graduate MFA program and author of "Starting with Goodbye", a novel published by University of Nevada Press.

CHAPTER 15

FAST BALLS, CURVES, AND DOG DAYS

By Kenneth V. Cummins

My Field of Dreams

I can still vividly recall that warm, sunny spring day in 1960, watching my brother out in the yard playing catch with Larry, a neighbor and friend of Bernie's who lived one mile to the west of our farm. Dad was in the shed working on his yellow Minneapolis Moline tractor.

"How did you do in the tryouts in town?" Bernie inquired of Larry as he tossed the baseball back to him.

"Struck out every batter," Larry beamed with a confident smile, as he fired the ball back toward Bernie with increasing speed, catching him by surprise. "By the end, I think they were getting afraid to face me. They were ducking out of the batter's box."

Larry was the hardest throwing right-hander my brother and I had shouldered a bat against, and neither of us was eager to watch that fastball rocket from his raised, hurling hand and speed toward home plate, a spherical blur heading straight toward you, or somewhere dangerously close.

"Well, don't throw me your fastball," Bernie teasingly implored. "I don't think I can handle it."

"What team did you get on?"

Larry's smile disappeared and his shoulders sagged. "None. After trying out, Mr. Coleman told me that to play on the town teams you had to live in town."

Dad was still focused on his tractor repairs, but I could tell he had been intently following the conversation between Bernie and Larry. "Like hell they have that rule!" he grumbled, fiercely hammering the tractor's hitch.

Decades before Kevin Costner made his beloved movie -- and 22 years before W. P. Kinsella penned his novel, *Shoeless Joe*, on which the beloved movie, *Field of Dreams*, is based -- my father, Bernard Cummins, created our own field of dreams in the pasture behind our south-central Kansas farm house to combat meaningless prejudice, right an injustice, and relive his own childhood dreams.

The next morning, Dad summoned Bernie and me to help him drag two big poles into the pasture near our house and set them yards apart in deep, hand-dug holes. Then we stretched layers of chicken wire between the poles. Dad ignored our questions about what we were building, but my brother and I were getting the idea. We were building a baseball diamond.

"Now," he announced when the backstop was complete, "this is home plate."

He traced the sacred spot with the toe of his left work boot. "Get the lawnmower and mow the infield and the base paths. Measure 90 feet straight this way and that's first base," Dad instructed, pointing to each location with the farmer's nod of the head. "Ninety feet over this way from there will be second base, and 90 feet down this way is third base."

The outfield would stay mostly un-mowed, which meant any ground ball hit through the mowed infield died quickly in the taller Johnson grass and milkweeds, making it difficult to hit ground-ball doubles and triples, as long as the outfielder could find the ball in the weeds fast enough.

Then Dad measured exactly 60 feet directly in front of home plate and in line with the second base location. "This is the pitcher's mound where Larry can fire his fastball."

All three of us eagerly set to work, but Dad seemed to be more excited than either Bernie or me. Growing up in Oklahoma, he was steeped in the mythology and lore of baseball and its deep infusion into the American character. To Dad, baseball was a rural game, played in sandlots and on make-shift fields just like the one he was preparing, and mastered by lanky, muscular country boys who had rare talents for hitting or hurling unhittable pitches. By all accounts, he was considered "a pretty good country ballplayer."

The New York Yankees homerun blaster Mickey Mantle, also an Oklahoma boy, and St. Louis Cardinals' pitching wizard Dizzy Dean were among his idols. On Saturday afternoons, I spent countless hours siting with Dad in front of the radio - and later the TV when we finally bought one - listening to Dizzy Dean sing *Wabash Cannonball* while announcing the "game of the week." The migration of the game from rural to urban and Caribbean locales had not yet accelerated in America, and baseball was still a game played in pastures just like ours, and played unusually well by country boys.

In one of my first memories of the numerous trips to my parents' homesteads northwest of Alva, Oklahoma, I was crammed in the backseat of our '54 Chevy between a beefy uncle and the husband of one of my Mom's numerous Hungarian sisters, who had sharp elbows and knees. Dad had two more of these specimens squeezed into the front seat next to him.

We drove on red dirt roads until finally coming to a stop at a pasture gate. The uncle on my right got out and opened the metal gate, and we proceeded across rolling, trackless pastureland where the grass had been eaten so close to the ground that the landscape looked like the green felt that covers snooker tables. I could not spot a house anywhere until we crested a steep hill and headed down into the valley. Halfway down the hill perched a small, solitary white frame house surrounded by sloping velvet-green pasture dotted with bristly shrubs.

We stopped at the front door and everyone squeezed out of the car and into the four-room, one-story house. Inside waited the former Sherriff for Woods County, Oklahoma, and I was eager to hear him tell of chasing the famous Bonnie and Clyde over these hills when the Barrow gang came through, stealing cars and robbing banks. One of Dad's former neighbors was so proud that Bonnie and Clyde chose his car to steal in their getaway that he always rooted for them to get away. He bragged about it for years. After all, the Barrows robbed banks, and that was fine with many people around there.

Dad and the uncles had heard that the sheriff was nearing the end of his trail, and they wanted to come see him one more time. He was in the back room sitting up in bed at 3 in the afternoon, appearing fully dressed, with a quilt thrown across his legs, sporting his large Stetson and facing the only window in the room. There was barely enough space for the visiting men to crowd in on both sides of the bed. I stood in the doorway, expectantly.

But the conversation from beginning to end was baseball, baseball, baseball. They talked about the hitting of Mantle, the fielding wizardry and base-running of Pepper Martin, the pitching prowess of Ralph Terry, and the diamond exploits of Alvin Dark; all rural and small-town Oklahoma boys who reached their destinies in professional baseball.

They also reminisced about local legends: John McGlothlin, who threw the best curveball they had ever seen, and who actually got called up by the St. Louis Cardinals, but suffered acute appendicitis his first season and never pitched again after a botched appendectomy. And Johnny so-and-so, who once hit a ball so hard and so far in the pasture field that it was never found, and the game had to be halted. No one else had brought a ball.

Poor Bonnie and Clyde; they never even got a mention.

By sundown on that Saturday Dad was creating or re-creating -- his field of dreams, we had completed our work, and all of us paused to look at the precious jewel we had just created out of the rough patch formerly known only as the bullpen pasture because it was used to separate bulls from the heifers, which also worked as a place where the bull pursued the fertile heifer who had little room to escape his advances.

"Tell all your friends, if they wanna play baseball, they have a place to come," Dad said, turning to walk back to the barn to begin the evening chores.

And come they did.

Saturday was game day at our diamond and we usually had more than 20 teenage boys show up. Each Saturday afternoon started with batting and fielding practice, with Dad coaching and hitting grounders and fly balls to the out fielders. When enough boys showed up, teams were chosen and a game ensued. After a few weeks, Dad convinced a neighbor -- who bought bulls from us from time to time and never paid his bill -- to get together his own team and play us on our field.

This neighbor had sons who were older than Bennie and me, so his team had older and bigger players. I was playing right field when one of those players, Jim Dorsey, hit a pitch so high and so far that I never found the ball in the tall grass. Two years later - after that supposed rule restricting the town teams to town kids was quietly and quickly forgotten - Jim played on a town team and was the first to hit a home run completely out of the town's sizable American Legion field. To this day, I have not heard of that feat being equaled.

Dad had a rule; every kid who showed up with a baseball glove got to play. Our second season, he managed to negotiate a schedule which had our team playing against the town teams, on their diamond, of course, Mulvane was only a town of 2,500 at the time (and not much more than that today), and was surrounded by wheat farms. But the town fathers still clung to their imagined caste system. They would never consent to letting their kids play baseball in a pasture, just as they resisted letting the farm kids take away team roster spots from their children.

Playing on their field was okay with us. The "stadium" behind the high school in town felt and looked more like a real baseball venue, and we were all happy to be competing there.

My hand-eye coordination suffered from a genetic eye condition, which made its appearance at the age of six, so baseball was never going to be a sport in which I could excel. But I soon became the leadoff batter. During one stretch in that second season, I led off and got on base 21 out of 22 times. The lone failure was a strikeout.

I didn't make contact with the baseball anywhere near as much as it made contact with me. Not always certain where the pitch was going, and having a tendency to crowd the plate, I either walked or got hit by the pitcher during those 21 successful at-bats.

Standing on first base, with the vast, slate gray sky at dusk arching over us like a protective shield, and a choir of locusts serenading the sun's diminish and fall, lights surrounding the field flickering on; listening to the chatter from comrades and competitors on the field and parents on the wooden bleachers; I was transported to a vanishing moment, another world existing and yet not-existing -- that only existed for that moment. It was a flat, wide world, a world filled with joy, adventure, achievement, daring, friendship, love.

Looking through the pitcher-catcher stare down to observe Dad standing on the other sideline, in his signature pinstriped bib overalls with the John Deere cap perched on his head, I could tell by the look on his face -- the same expression I imagined I bore at that moment -- that he was moving somewhere in time, maybe back, maybe ahead. Wherever he was, he was reliving memories and feelings from his childhood and growing up years, and cherishing the mythology of baseball that developed around him since then. He looked younger, more animated and reinvigorated from the labors of tending a wheat and cattle farm, and working a second job in the aircraft industry. In those moments -- standing on the sidelines yelling encouragement to his batters and pitchers, signaling his coaches at third and first, watching his players become more skilled in the game he loved, he was transferring that love to another generation.

In those moments, we were both connected to everyone who had played the game of baseball in the past, and everyone, boys and now girls, who will play it in the future: Every youngster who experiences the joy of swinging the bat and feeling it change the direction of the pitch; every young outfielder making a running catch of a hard-hit ball; every batter watching the ball come off his bat and elude the infielders or escape the gloves of the racing outfielders or sail over the outfield fence; every infielder starting or completing a double play, every runner sliding safely into home base, avoiding the catcher's tag; to score the winning run in the bottom of the ninth. The connection, once made, is never broken.

I took a few steps away from first base and watched the pitcher stare at me, foolishly thinking, perhaps, that I was going to steal. I listened to our first base coach quietly muttering base-running instructions in my ear. I saw the batter swing and heard the whack of wood connecting with rawhide. I followed the flight of the baseball into the outfield and away from the fielder as I raced toward second base. I glanced toward third, where the neighbor who didn't pay for his cows was coaching for Dad, and quickly heeded his right arm frantically waving wheeling, the signal to keep running. Sliding successfully into third base, I stood triumphantly on the bag, eager to score the first run of the game.

Our field of dreams lasted only a few years. The teams in town pilfered all of our best players, and the prejudice that had sparked the creation of the field had dissipated. But those who played and watched on that bullpen field have never forgotten those moments. At Dad's memorial service in 2008, some of those players returned to recount the memories he had made possible for them five decades earlier.

Our neighbor two miles to the east had three sons who played on the team. Their father also farmed by day and worked in the aircraft industry at night, and he counted on his sons to handle a good portion of the workload on the farm. But he did let them off on Saturdays, and later on game nights during the week, to play baseball.

"Your Dad gave my brothers their childhood," their sister observed years later.

Baseball may no longer be the country's most popular sport. Football, with all of its vulgarities, has taken over that spot. But no other sport can claim to be so imbedded in the history, culture and character of the country. No other sport fosters and maintains the mythology of baseball. No other sport has Presidents clamoring to throw out the first pitch each season. It is truly American.

Play ball.

Yes, Dogs Have Souls!

"Do dogs have souls?" a parishioner at St. Raphael Catholic Church asked Father Mike Salah during the weekly Saturday morning men's fellowship breakfast.

"Of course dogs have souls," Father Mike Salah responded without any hesitation, and with conviction. "Their souls are not the same as people's souls, but, yes dogs have souls, too."

Anyone who has been a dog owner, and rescued a dog from abuse and abandonment, will testify to that.

Mindy Farber in Potomac devotes her time and energy -- as well as that of her husband -- to rescuing dogs from the crowded Cumberland animal shelter many miles away in western Maryland.

For months, she had worked to rescue Sandy, a pit bull mix, from being euthanized. Finding Sandy a home was going to take a miracle. Sandy looked so sad, beaten down and miserable. His skin sagged, his eyes drooped, he was terribly underweight and would not eat, and he had the look of a dog who had completely given up on human kindness.

He also had injuries from being thrown from the back of a speeding pickup truck by his former owner. Placing dogs in open pickup truck beds and then speeding and swerving around until they are tossed out seems to be a sport among testosterone-overburdened males. My daughter rescued a small poodle mix who had suffered the same fate in North Carolina.

Sandy's execution was scheduled many times, and each time, Mindy managed to get it postponed. She was like the lawyer petitioning the Supreme Court at the eleventh hour before the death-row prisoner was scheduled to die at the hands of the State.

Finally, it seemed Sandy's stays of execution had been exhausted, and he was going to be put down within hours. But, miraculously, Mindy found a family in Potomac, with three rescue dogs already, willing to bet on Sandy.

A few weeks later, Mindy posted a picture of Sandy in his new home. He was unrecognizable from his former, forlorn photo. Sandy's smile could not have been any wider without splitting his skull. He looked livelier, healthier and genuinely happy again with his new life. His soul had been reawakened by human affection.

My friend Vince cannot recall his last hours with his small husky, Boo, twenty five years before without breaking down completely. Boo, who had grown old and frail and suffering failing body organs, would be put to sleep the next morning. Vince spent that night lying on the floor next to Boo, with his arms wrapped lovingly around his dying friend.

A similar farewell moment between dog and man was depicted later in the film, *Marley and Me,* which left every child moviegoer exiting the cinema weeping uncontrollably, and some adults, too.

Jerry still becomes teary-eyed when he recalls a moment with his black and white lab mix, Teddy, which happened nearly a half century earlier. Jerry was coming home from an extended hospital stay after heart surgery. As he exited his car and began to trudge toward his front door, there was Teddy waiting eagerly in the open doorway, not rushing out as he had been trained not to do, but bouncing eagerly from leg to leg at the sight of his companion's return after the long, unexplained absence.

President Harry S. Truman famously and cynically once proclaimed: "If you want a friend in Washington, get a dog!" And just about every president in my lifetime has, except Donald Trump.

There is no friendship greater than that between a dog and his or her companion. Dogs convey the unconditional love that Jesus implored his disciples to show to their fellow humans.

Every time I encounter Mike, he recounts the last moments of Murphy, his poodle. Mike had resisted pressure from his children and wife to put the aging poodle to sleep because of the pain his dog obviously was in. Finally, he agreed to get the deed done.

Once Murphy was on the vet's table and looking away, Mike thought he could slip out the door but as he looked back before exiting, Murphy stared directly into his eyes. "That look is gonna haunt me the rest of my life," Mike mourned.

Outside, Mike changed his mind, and rush back in. But the vet had already used his needle, and Murphy was gone.

When we had to put down Reese - our beagle/black-and-tan coon hound with a bit of Rottweiler -- I was surprised at how hard it hit me. I grew up on a Kansas farm and accustomed to seeing the pet dog run over by the neighbor's sand truck, or shot after he started running with a pack of farm dogs and chasing cattle at night, or killed by coyotes. I approached Reese's pending demise after 12 years with us with nonchalance. But that morning, my emotions fell in on me like a collapsing building, and my entire body ached. My heart was shattering.

It was finally time; and yet, was it really time? Were we exaggerating her pain and her decline? No. But I couldn't stop grasping for reasons to stop this. We made Reese comfortable on the couch and were feeding her bits of the forbidden chocolate as fast as she could eat them while we said our goodbyes.

Finally, the vet moved forward and sank the needle in, Reese drifted off immediately, lowering her head onto her front paws, her eyes closed and a peaceful look spreading over her face. She was gone from us.

After that, home had an emptiness that hurt our souls. A family member had departed, only her ashes remained. We discussed waiting at least six months before deciding whether to get another dog, but the emptiness and loneliness was overbearing, and not going away. After 10 weeks, we began the search for a new dog, and soon rescued a mostly white-pointer/Dalmatian mix. We named her Betty White in honor of Betty White, who had passed away during our search. Betty White was not yet a year old when she was rescued from the streets of Harlingen, Texas -- an area, along with the South, where there is an over-supply of strays and shelter dogs -- and shipped to Maryland, where the demand is seemingly insatiable.

Finding a dog more loveable and in need of love, than Betty White, would be an impossible feat.

Dogs are smart, gentle, faithful, loving, devoted, and non-judgmental.

Yes, dogs have souls. Big souls!

Man's Best Friend

Piper shivered in his cage, his legs trembling, paws moving up and down on the shelter's cold, concrete floor. Tears of despair and abandonment flowed from his half-shut eyes. He could see the other dogs casting him looks of disapproval from their own identical, confining steel prisons strewn across the warehouse floor. Try as he might, he could not hold back the tears, nor quell the whimpers rising up from deep within his small, black-and-white border collie frame.

"C'mon. Dog up!" barked Pug, a boxer-bulldog mix. "You act like you've never been in a shelter before."

"I . . . I never have," Piper whimpered. "I have lived for ten years with John, and he was very kind and loving to me. He and Wendy took good care of me, and I was devoted to them, especially John. I never slept anywhere but in my bed in John's house, next to his bed, and sometimes in bed with him.

"Until tonight."

"Well, where is wonderful John now?" piped up Kogo, joining Pug in disapproval of Piper's display of weakness.

"A truck with flashing lights came one night and took Wendy away," Piper answered softly. "Two men rolled her out on a bed, and I never saw her again. John was very sad for a long time. It was just John and me in the house, and I tried very hard every day to cheer him up."

Piper paused. From every cage around him, he could feel the eyes of the abandoned dogs inside focused intently on him, waiting for him to continue.

"Then Gloria moved in," Piper began again, breaking the silence, "and John seemed so-ooo so happy again. They both had shiny new rings on their fingers. But I could tell from the start that Gloria didn't like me. Today, when John was at work, she brought me here and left me."

"She told them I eat too much food," Piper said, somewhat embarrassed.

"Anybody wanna' bet that marriage is gonna' last?" quipped Leonard, a golden retriever and Labrador mix.

253

"I only ate the food put out for me," Piper said sheepishly, feeling the need to defend himself. "I wasn't getting into cupboards or up on tables eating food I wasn't supposed to."

The other dogs listening to and watching Piper were becoming less disparaging of him.

"Aw, it's not so bad here," consoled Imogene, a Chihuahua and poodle mix. "At least you're not out there."

Piper turned to follow Imogene's nose pointed at the window where icy raindrops pelted the outside pane separating the shelter's dimly-lit interior from the impenetrable darkness beyond. The rain and sleet tapped out staccato melody on the shelter's corrugated tin roof.

"Yeah. Chimed in Rocky, a Saint Bernard mixed with . . . well . . . no one was quite sure what. "Many of us were strays on the streets until we were picked up and brought up here with about a hundred dogs in one bus. It was warmer down south than here, so life on the street was not so awful, except it was lonely, and hard to find food. It's freezing here in western Maryland."

"I didn't want to say anything, but you all sound different when you talk," Piper offered, the canine conversation easing his loneliness. "Where are you from?"

"Georgia."

"South Carolina."

"North Carolina."

"Texas."

Each of the 13 dogs yelled out his or her birth place.

"You've never heard that southern and western dog drawl before?" Leonard asked gently. "There are so many dogs running loose where some of us came from that they ship us up here where rescue dogs are scarce and the human demand for companionship is high."

"They like to call us Man's Best Friend," Rocky barked in, "but man doesn't always treat us that way. Take Kogo over there."

Piper looked into the cage in the far corner of the room and at the slumped, motionless and silent lump of spaniel and terrier mix inside.

"His owner put him in the back of his pickup truck and drove around wildly until Kogo was tossed out onto the concrete, and then just kept going."

Others in the shelter began sharing similar tales of neglect. The dogs chattered back and forth, and the strange place seemed less lonely and foreboding to Piper.

Soon the chatter turned to playful banter.

"Don't waste your time on Imogene over there," quipped Sugar, a member of the potcake breed. "She's gay."

"I am not!" Imogene barked, springing up on all four legs glaring at Sugar.

"Well, I never see you hangin' around with any of us male dogs. You don't date, and you've never had any puppies."

"You've got some nerve!" Imogene growled as she sank back down to the cold floor and buried her head between her front paws.

"Look who's talkin'?" Buddy, a young, French bulldog yelped in. "You're a boy and you're named Sugar."

"It's pronounced Shuga. S H U G A! I'm from the islands," Sugar protested.

"Yeah. Right." Buddy smirked, rolling his eyes while glancing at each occupied cage.

Suddenly, the cold and darkness was interrupted by bright light, and the small door beyond the cages opened. All of the dogs pushed to the front of their cages and barked gleefully as Maya, a favorite on the shelter's staff, entered and was heading toward Piper's cage. She patted every upturned nose pressed through small openings as she passed.

At Piper's cage, the young, slight, dog whisperer knelt and eyed the Border collie sympathetically. "Hang on, Piper," she said softly. "We are going to get you out of here."

Maya rose and walked quickly to the door, yanked it open and exited.

"You're in luck," Leonard assured Piper. "She doesn't think you belong here, either, and she's going to find you a home."

Maya took the light with her when she left. The dogs soon quieted down in the darkness after her departure, and soft snoring was the only sound disrupting the silence.

Piper continued to shiver through the night, never quite sure if he was awake or sleeping, in the present or the past. Spacious back yards with soft grass and inhabited by friendly dogs, long walks on leashes in the woods, energetic moments with squeaky toys rolled past in his vision. A bright light was coming toward him.

Piper opened his eyes and there was Maya again, opening his cage. The other dogs were all awake and yelping encouragement in their excitement.

Maya slipped a leash over his head and gently led him toward the door.

"Way to go Piper! You're getting out of here," barked Imogene.

"Maya found you a home," Leonard assured.

At the door, Piper stopped and looked back, feeling a moment of guilt and sadness that he was leaving and his new-found friends had to stay behind.

Then he turned and walked into the sunlight, never looking back.

At the Mailbox

Dad crossed the gravel road that runs past our driveway, on his way to check the mailbox, when Earl, our neighbor two miles to the east, was passing and halted his car to talk.

"Hi, Bernard."

"Hey Earl. Wha'd'ya know?"

"I know for damn sure I am going to start locking my doors at night after what happened to that Clutter family in Holcomb. Hell, we never lock our doors. Nobody's home right now and the doors are unlocked. You just never think something like that could happen. I'm on my way to town to get some groceries Connie needs."

"Yeah, we leave everything unlocked around here, even when we go into Wichita for the day. It's a damn shame, entire family murdered in cold blood like that. And for what? Fifty dollars and a pair of binoculars!

"Don't make any sense." He looked away into the cloudy midday sky.

I moved slowly around the cedar tree in our yard by the road, wanting to get closer to hear them talk without being noticed so that Dad and Earl didn't change their conversation. They were recounting the gruesome murders of four members of the Herbert Clutter family - father, wife and two teenage children - nearly 250 miles distant from our comfortable, welcoming rural community, but a community that was the carbon copy of the one the Clutters lived in.

The murders had sent tremors of fear throughout the entire state of Kansas and, eventually much of the nation. I didn't know it then, as I listened in on that late November day in 1959, but these murders, the trial and execution of the two killers, Truman Capote's harrowing account in his bestselling book, *In Cold Blood*, and the movie based on the book, would keep the horror alive and present for the next 10 years, and would forever change the behaviors of rural and small-town residents. Few would go to bed at night after that without locking their doors, and many even started locking their cars. The era of feeling safe and immune from evil was ending.

At the mailbox was where the men in our community preferred to talk. Neighbors would often stop on the road at the end of our driveway, not bothering to come into the farmyard, and Dad would walk out to greet them. This was their private place to converse. The men almost never talked to each other on the phone, unless it was an emergency to report that a neighboring farmer, or member of his family, had been injured, or killed, in a farm accident. Even in those rare instances of phone communication, the male caller would not convey distressing news to my Mom; she always had to go outside and find Dad to come take the call.

Our phone system was a party line, eight families on the same hookup. Every time one of the eight got a call, the seven others heard the ring in their homes. But phone etiquette forbade eavesdropping on the conversation of others. Etiquette was not always observed.

Three short rings on the huge, wooden-box telephone mounted on the wall in the hallway meant that someone on the party line, or outside, was trying to reach us. The rings would sound through the two large bells, covered by silver metal cones, at the top of the phone box. Lifting the heavy cylindrical earpiece from its cradle on the left side of the wooden box allowed you to hear the caller. Speaking into the mouthpiece that jutted out half a foot from the front of the phone box enabled the caller to hear you. The small handle on the right side of the box was used to make calls. The specific ring of each family on the party line would alert that party of a call from a neighbor. One long ring connected you to the operator, who would handle calls outside the party line. When you got an incoming "long- distance" call, the operator connected you, and she could discreetly listen to the call, if she succumbed to temptation.

The women on our party line didn't seem to mind that much if someone was listening in. "I could hear Mildred pick up the phone as soon as Elsie and I started talking," Mom would often say after a phone conversation, referring to our immediate neighbor to the west. Mom and her sister would switch to their native Hungarian tongue when they suspected an eavesdropper was on the line.

But the men avoided the telephone, preferring to talk in their special place at the mailbox.

"They woke old man Clutter up and then slit his throat and shot him in the head," Earl continued on that November day light years ago, retelling the gruesome details. "Then they shot his wife and killed the two kids, who were about the same age as my Darrel and Elaine."

"What kind of person would do that, especially to those kids?" Dad wondered sadly, shaking his head and looking off again to the horizon.

Just then, Howard, our mail carrier, arrived and stopped parallel to Earl's car, with Dad standing between the two cars. The road now was completely blocked for traffic in both directions, but it was not likely another car would be approaching anytime soon.

"You fellas talkin' 'bout those murders of that Clutter family?" Howard inquired as he handed Dad a sheaf of mail -- the local weekly newspaper with a couple of letters stuck inside -- through his open car window.

"Yeah" Dad answered. "Such a damn shame. Have you heard any news, Howard?"

"Heard they're lookin' for two fellows who got out of prison in Lansing. They thought old man Clutter kept a lot of money in a safe in his home. That was the talk in the prison. When they found out there was no safe full of money in the house, they went crazy and wiped out the whole family."

"Doesn't make sense that a rich guy like that would have his money in his home; he'd be keeping his money in the local bank," Earl observed. "He might even have been on the board of the bank in town."

"They are still on the loose," Howard continued. "Police don't know where they are. They could be in Mexico by now. I'd be surprised if they were still in the state. Everyone is on the lookout now."

"Well, I gotta go," Howard said, shifting his brand new Chevrolet Impala into gear. "People are waiting on their mail."

"Keep your doors locked," he advised as he departed.

"So long, Howard," Dad replied.

"I've gotta go, too," Earl said. "Connie's waiting on her groceries."

"Yeah, I've got to get to workin' on the tractor," Dad said. "It hasn't been runnin' right. May be a bad plug or piston."

"See ya' later Bernard."

"Take it easy, Earl."

My world, and the world I would come to inhabit, began changing that day. Evil and fear had intruded into what had been an idyllic and innocent life for my first ten years.

The capture, trial, and executions of the two murderers, and the retelling of the horrors, consumed much of my early life. After the Clutter murders came the Vietnam War, the military draft lottery, high school and college classmates dying in a faraway war, the beatings and killings of civil rights workers, the Manson murders in Los Angeles, seat belts, motorcycle helmets, 55 miles per hour speed limits, the senseless and horrifying reign of terror of the BTK serial killer in Wichita, airplane hijackings, the massacre of Congressman Leo Ryan and his party at the Jonestown settlement in Guyana, AIDS, space shuttle disasters, the U.S. government's slaughter of families at the Branch Davidian camp in Waco, Texas, the 9/11 attack on the World Trade Center that took nearly 3,000 lives, the endless wars in Iraq and Afghanistan, annoying security procedures at airports, the coronavirus lockdown, the violent January 6 insurrection at the U.S. Capitol to stop the peaceful transfer of power, mass school shootings, the proliferation of gun ownership in the U.S. amounting to more than one gun for every man, woman and child of any age.

Each episode magnified the fear and deepened the numbness; and resulted in new restrictions intended to make us feel safe and more secure in a seemingly ever-more dangerous world. But what have we gained in our voluntary acceptance of the continuing quest to construct a safer and saner world? And what have we given up? Or lost?

No one gathers at the mailbox anymore. The red metal flag on the side of the silver box -- a signal to the mailman to stop and collect the letters to be mailed inside -- is almost never raised anymore. The flags have become rusted in their down positions on the side of the box with the silver paint chipping away. Now, people drive their mailings to the local post office, believing it will have a better chance of reaching its destination - and sooner - if deposited there. And the mailman seldom has to stop on his rural route to put mail in the box. The Internet, email, online shopping, and bill-paying have reduced his load to commercial and political mailers that get discarded before read.

Gone is the every-day joy of heading to the mailbox nailed to the post cemented into the old, iron milk can on the roadside to see what surprises it may contain.

The clunky box phone on the wall has been replaced by ones carried in pockets that can track every move we make and action we take, and creates the stifling expectation we are willing to be interrupted at any minute of the day. As an octogenarian friend recently observed in frustration: "I got this damn iPhone. Now everyone wants to call me!"

Much has been gained, and much has been lost.

The farmers and neighbors in my former rural home community spend their days in solitary confinement in their tractors in dusty crop fields, or in their cars alone going somewhere they went the day before, and the week before, and the week before that. Or they work at noisy jobs in the aircraft industry and seldom speak to another person for eight hours every day.

We live in a much more connected and populated world, but many of us seem much more desperately and painfully alone.

Alone, but fears persist.

High School Albatross

No one ever forgets their high school years, no matter how long a life lived, or how far the distance traveled from those moments. For some, high school represents an awakening -- a blossoming of skills and forging of friendships that form a sturdy foundation for lifelong expansion and achievements.

For others, it was a time best forgotten -- but can't be: a time of sexual awkwardness, competition, longing to be popular; a time of feeling unappreciated, hemmed in; a time of not being able to find the right footing for the life yet to be experienced.

Bobby Keys (1943-2014) was the greatest rock 'n' roll sax player of all time. He traveled far from his small hometown of Slaton, Texas, population 6,000, then and now. He toured the U.S. and the world with legendary singers and bands, including Buddy Holly, Rolling Stones, Joe Cocker, George Harrison, and John Lennon.

But he was never able to bring himself to set foot back in his high school. No one knows the reason because Bobby never said why he couldn't perform this simple act on a very small stage. The scars of high school never healed.

Bobby came close to getting back into Slaton High. He traveled all the way there for his 50th high school class reunion, but never got out of his car, parked on the street outside the school building. "No one in there is going to remember me," he lamented, while sitting in that car and looking longingly at his old school. After two hours of hesitation, he drove away, and flew back to Europe to rejoin the Stones on tour.

A short time later, the Lord called Bobby home, as they say in Texas.

Bobby Keys could stand before huge stadium crowds and pour his soul into memorable solos on numerous hit songs, including the Stones' *Brown Sugar* and Lennon's *Whatever Gets You Through the Night*. But he couldn't face being forgotten in his hometown.

Even Jesus taught his disciples that a prophet has no honor in his native place, and has to go elsewhere to be appreciated.

♦ ♦ ♦ ♦ ♦

About the Author

Born in Northwest Kalama in 1949, Kenneth Cummins left before the age of three when his family moved to Kansas. His Sooner state ties led him to the writings and philosophies of Will Rogers and Woody Guthrie. From an early age, he yearned to be a writer, but settled on journalism, thinking it wouldn't require as much imagination.

A 1972 journalism graduate of the University of Kansas, Kenneth came to Washington D.C. in 1976 to pursue passions for investigative and political reporting. He has worked and written for the Chicago Tribune, The Washington Post, Washington Monthly, New Republic, Washingtonian, Reader's Digest, and Washington City Paper (creator of the Loose Lips column).

He founded and managed a Private Investigator firm for 30 years, which cured his lack of imagination.

Made in the USA
Middletown, DE
08 October 2022

12306771R00157